# Alpha, Beta and Omega

Greta Sullivan

Copyright © 2024 by Greta Sullivan

All rights reserved.

No portion of this book may be reproduced in any form without written permission from the publisher or author, except as permitted by U.S. copyright law.

# contents

| | |
|---|---|
| Chapter One | 1 |
| Chapter Two | 6 |
| Chapter Three | 12 |
| Chapter Four | 16 |
| Chapter Five | 22 |
| Chapter Six | 28 |
| Chapter Seven | 34 |
| Chapter Eight | 39 |
| Chapter Nine | 43 |
| Chapter Ten | 48 |
| Chapter Eleven | 54 |
| Chapter Twelve | 59 |
| Chapter Thirteen | 64 |

| | |
|---|---|
| Chapter Fourteen | 70 |
| Chapter Fifteen | 75 |
| Chapter Sixteen | 81 |
| Chapter Seventeen | 85 |
| Chapter Eighteen | 89 |
| Chapter Nineteen | 96 |
| Chapter Twenty | 102 |
| Chapter Twenty-One | 109 |
| Chapter Twenty-Two | 114 |
| Epilogue | 121 |

# Chapter One

It was raining when Kali woke up.

The soft pitter patter of it hitting the bedroom window was almost enough to lure her back to sleep. But then she heard the familiar sound of high heels on the hallway floor just outside her bedroom door. The scent of bubblegum perfume drifting through the wood of the door and further confirming who was heading downstairs. Her elder sister, Chloe.

Grumbling faintly she pulled a pillow over her head, wondering what on earth had Chloe up and out of bed at...she peeked at her alarm clock...seven in the morning. Chloe was not known as a morning person. Then again Kali wasn't exactly a morning person herself but at least she had a reason to be up. Which meant she couldn't just roll over and go back to sleep. With a soft sigh she pushed the pillow off her head and sat up, kicking the blanket away before swinging her legs over the edge of the bed.

She yawned sleepily as she stretched, her muscles shifting and settling before she stood, crossing the room to her dresser, sitting in the desk chair that should really have been in the corner at her desk, grabbing up her brush before attempting to tame the wildness that was her wavy and curly hair. It would never lie completely straight, not like Chloe's, but once it was brushed out it did hang rather nicely around her pale, heart shaped face. Looking in the mirror, studying her reflection she tried to see what everyone else in the pack saw.

The oddball. The girl who didn't fit in.

Too docile, they said when they thought she couldn't hear them. Too calm for a she-wolf. Especially for a daughter of a Beta.

She couldn't help it if she was more passive than other wolves.

She couldn't help it if she would submit instead of fight.

It was just who she was.

Her mother tried to reassure her that there was nothing wrong with her, that the gods didn't make everyone the same and they had made her just the way she was meant to be. Too bad that the rest of the pack, her sister included, didn't share that view. They were all certain that there was something wrong with her. Chloe had even started calling her a freak when they were kids.

Sighing softly she quickly pinned her hair up in a ponytail, putting on the mask she wore, just in order to get through the day. Standing once more she hurriedly got dressed, black sneakers, dark jeans and a white t-shirt, pretty standard clothing for working at the town's only bookstore. Glancing back at the mirror as she picked up her jacket and shoulder bag she saw someone who didn't stand out. Someone who blended into the background. Better than standing out and drawing attention to herself.

She'd learned in junior high school just how bad that was.

Sighing again she left her room and slipped as quietly as she could down the hallway and stairs, entering the kitchen just in time to hear Chloe's loud complaint.

"But daddy! The purse only costs, like, three hundred dollars."

Apparently their father had said no to some new designer handbag. Surprising. Since he usually always gave into Chloe's demands. For her sixteenth birthday their father had purchased her a car. A little silver Audi convertible that Chloe had gushed and gushed about for months. When Kali turned sixteen, just two years after Chloe, their father had purchased her a bicycle. With a basket. "It suits you, honey." Their father had said as she'd stood and stared at the dark red bicycle, all while Chloe snickered in the background.

"Chloe, for the last time," their father, Martin, snapped from where he sat at the kitchen table, flipping through the local paper. "I'm not giving you six hundred dollars for a purse when you just got a new one last month."

Chloe made a low sound, growling faintly, storming from the kitchen, shoving Kali aside as she went, giving her a nasty look before disappearing down the hall. Kali watched her sister go before she quickly crossed the kitchen, snagging an apple from the bowl on the table.

"Working, Kali?"

Her father didn't look up from the paper as he spoke.

"It's my day to open," she said softly, setting her purse down long enough to shrug into her jacket and pull her hood up, tucking the apple into her shoulder bag as she slung the strap over her head, letting the bag rest against her side. "And to close. So I'll probably be home late."

A low hum of acknowledgment followed by a simple statement of "It's a full moon tonight."

She paused by the door to the garage, looking back at her father, who still hadn't looked up from the paper. "I know," she said calmly, though part of her was freaking out. She hated full moons. She absolutely hated them. Three nights every month when the pack would run together. And she always had to run alone. "I'll be home before the meeting. I promise."

Another hum of acknowledgment but nothing else.

She didn't say goodbye as she slipped out, grabbing her bicycle from where she left it leaning against the garage wall, sliding silently and carefully by Chloe's car. Stepping out into the rain she found it was falling fairly steadily, meaning it probably wouldn't let up as the day progressed. Sighing softly she climbed onto her bicycle and headed off down the street towards the bookstore.

She had a feeling that it was going to be a long day.

## Chapter Two

By the time Kali reached the bookstore the rain had let off a bit, enough to suggest that perhaps it would stop before the afternoon. Going around the back of the old brick building she left her bicycle by the back stairs, chaining it to the metal handrail before she climbed the steps, fishing a set of keys from her shoulder bag. Once she was inside she turned off the alarm and headed for the break room, turning on the lights as she passed the switches. Entering the break room she turned on the lights before pulling her shoulder bag off, hanging it on a peg by the window. She was just shrugging out of her jacket when she heard the back door open and then hurried footsteps. "Kali?" "Break room, Amy," she called over her shoulder as she hung her jacket up on the same peg as her bag, turning just as Amy came sliding into the break room, sneakers no doubt soaked. "Shit!" Amy barely managed to catch her balance and Kali couldn't help but grin as the other girl held her arms out at her sides, using them like a pole to adjust her balance. Amy grinned as she looked at Kali. It was a look of triumph. "And that is how it's done!"Kali laughed as she shook her head as Amy continued to grin while shoving her multicoloured hair out of her face. Kali crossed the room in a few quick strides and turned on the coffee maker. "You won't be saying that when your butt hits the floor.""Naw." Amy waved her hand absently, pulling her jacket off and hanging it on the peg next to Kali's. "When it happens I'll just spring back to my feet and pretend it never happened.""Just like when we were children." "Exactly!"Kali laughed again."Keep an eye on the coffee maker, will you?" Kali headed for the door. "I need to go unlock the front."Amy saluted her and Kali laughed as she made her way through the store, checking a few stacks of new books as she passed them, unlocking the front door quickly and turning the sign to read open before turning and making her way over to the counter, stepping around it and booting up the computer. A few clicks of the mouse later and everything was up and running before she unlocked the till, checking that the usual amount of money was still in it before sliding the drawer shut once more.She had just tucked the keys into her pocket when Amy set a cup of coffee on the counter in front of her. "You look like you need it," Amy said with a shrug, holding her own cup. "Because, and no offense, you look like crap."Kali rolled her eyes, picking up her cup and taking a sip, thankful that Amy had only put in one spoon of sweetener. "Long night."Amy took a big swig of her coffee, making an affirmative sound around her mouthful, swallowing loudly. "Figured that out for meself, thanks much," she quipped as she hopped up and sat on the counter. "Want to share the reason why it was so long?" Kali turned her cup in her hands, looking down at the brown liquid. "I had that dream again." Amy's eyebrows shot up, surprise written all over her face, even as she studied Kali curiously. "Again? That's, what, the third time this week?" "Sixth." Amy let out a low whistle. "Damn, that's..." She hesitated, clearly searching for the right word. "That's whacked." Kali snorted as she took another sip of coffee. "That's one way of putting it." "But...I mean...it's just a dream, right?" Kali shrugged. "If you'd have asked me six months ago I'd have said yes but...but this is getting nuts. The same dream? Exactly the same dream? And now it's getting to be nearly every night?" Amy shrugged and tipped her head to one side, causing her hair to slip over her shoulder, which made her look so much younger than she was. "Well," she said as the bell over the front door jingled, causing her to hop off the counter. "I'm sure it doesn't mean anything, Kal. Just a dream." Kali smiled and nodded. "Right," she replied as Mrs Vestaburg came walking towards the counter. "Just a dream." Amy gave a nod before moving off towards the back of the store. Kali turned her attention to Mrs Vestaburg. "Good morning, Mrs Vestaburg, can I help you?" oOoOoOoBy the time lunch rolled around Kali was never so happy to turn the sign on the door to Out to Lunch, Back By One. The morning had been insane, people rushing in and out to collect books they'd special orders. A few just popping in to browse the shelves and even one girl who'd been torn between what type of Renaissance art books she wanted. Kali had tried to help each and every customer to the best of her abilities but when most everyone was giving her sideways glances when they thought she wasn't looking it became tedious rather quickly. Shaking her head as she headed for the break room, hearing the radio that Amy had already turned on, she smiled as she stepped into the break room finding Amy lounging on the sofa with a tuna sandwich and bottle of lime soda. "You call that lunch," she teased as she went to where her shoulder bag was and fished out her apple. "Better than that!" Amy pointed at the apple with the corner of her sandwich, nose wrinkling slightly. "Seriously, Kal, that is not a proper lunch." Kali rolled her eyes and went to the little cupboard above the counter where the coffee maker and microwave sat. She reached up and fetched a bag of chips and chocolate cookies that she'd tucked away behind a large can of instant coffee, shaking both at Amy who grinned like a loon. "Woman after my own heart," Amy said as Kali walked over, sitting on the floor by the sofa, leaning back against the cushions and Amy's legs. They ate in comfortable silence for a little while before Kali broke it. "Did you hear about the new pack over in Lawton?" Amy made a low, affirmative sound, chewing a bite of sandwich thoroughly before swallowing and speaking. "Heard my Mum and Aunt Carol talking about it." She wiped her mouth with the back of her hand.

"Think it's odd, the Council letting a new pack set up so close to us. I mean, Lawton's only a twenty minute drive away. That's...That's insanely close." Kali nodded. "Heard my dad say that most of the pack is from the United Kingdom." "Seriously?" Kali nodded and Amy made a loud sound. "Wonder why they came across the pond." "Dad says that Benjamin said the Lawton Alpha has connections in the Council." Amy snorted. "Snobby bastard. Probably a great big bunch of prissy shits." Kali chuckled and took a bite of her apple, chewing slowly. "Been meaning to ask, Ames," she said, taking another bite out of her apple, talking around it. "Haws bated lipe?" Amy laughed, sipping her soda, before answering. "Mated life is just fantastic, thanks." Kali chuckled, swallowing quickly, and looking up at her best friend. "So you and Roy are all rainbows and sunshine?" Amy rolled her eyes as she reached down and smacked Kali's shoulder playfully. "Roy and I are fine," she said as she snatched the cookie bag and opened it, snagging a few before setting it on the floor next to Kali. "We have our moments, like every mated couple I suppose, but it's been good. I feel...whole. In a way I haven't felt before." Kali smiled, looking at her half eaten apple. "I'm really happy for you," she said as she looked at Amy, still smiling, letting her head rest against Amy's knee. "Hey," Amy nudged her gently, affectionately, a pack mate comforting another. "You'll find your mate. Just you wait and see. You're going to go back to college in the fall and you'll be walking down the street some sunny afternoon and you'll see him, or her, and you'll just...you'll know, ya know?" Kali smiled as she rubbed her cheek against Amy's knee. "What's it like? Meeting your mate?" Amy sighed almost wistfully. "It's like...It's like the excitement of Christmas and your birthday wrapped up with this...this feeling of utter contentment and peace and love and...and..." She broke off for a moment, clearly trying to find the right words but before she could the bell over the front door jingled and they both jumped, surprised, since no one in town usually came into the store when the sign said Out To Lunch. "Hello?" A rich, masculine voice called out and Kali glanced towards the break room. "Anyone here?" Kali and Amy exchanged identical looks before they spoke in unison. "It's your turn!"

## Chapter Three

"I dealt with Mr Goldman," Kali said quickly, before Amy could protest or convince her to go deal with the customer. "For nearly an hour, I dealt with him, and I know he thinks I'm some sort of freak. He mutters about it often enough. So, you," she poked Amy in the knee. "Can go out there and deal with whoever has come to interrupt our lunch hour." Amy whined softly but before she could form some sort of argument the man called out again. "Hello?" Amy sighed. "Fine," she grumbled, climbing from the sofa carefully so she didn't end up kicking Kali or anything. "But you owe me." Kali saluted her just as the man called out again, which made Amy roll her eyes and shout, "Be right with you, sir." She gave Kali a look that clearly said is this idiot serious? which made Kali snicker as she watched Amy walk from the room with a huff of breath. Normally she would have listened to the conversation, a perk of being a wolf, but today she just closed her eyes and leaned back against the sofa, enjoying a moment of quiet before it was broken by Amy's loud shout."Hey, Kal! Guy's looking for a copy of William Blake's Songs of Innocence and Experience. Says he called earlier."Kali sighed and pushed herself to her feet, knowing that Amy would pretend not to find it even if she told her friend where she'd put the book after the man had called inquiring if they had a copy. All because the man had interrupted their lunch break. Amy liked little revenges like that.Dropping her half eaten apple into the rubbish bin she walked out into the store, smiling as she slipped between the stacks and headed for the counter. Amy was standing behind it, looking rather annoyed but trying to seem like a cheerful employee of the book store, while the customer leaned against the counter, clearly waiting as patiently as he could.Kali spared him a glance as she passed, slipping around the counter. His hair was dark and curly, falling just to his shoulders. His face, angular but not sharp, bore a five o'clock shadow and he was smirking slightly, eyes hidden behind a dark pair of sunglasses. His posture spoke of a relaxed, if somewhat impatient, man. But Kali saw the tension in his shoulders. The way he turned his head subtly, looking towards the door as though expecting someone, before he looked back at Amy.Without a word she reached beneath the counter and set the copy of Songs of Innocence and Experience on the counter, looking at Amy she gave a soft smile. Amy huffed as Kali patted her arm, stepping away and around the counter."Thanks, Kali," Amy called after her and she merely waved, heading over to straighten up a stack of the latest Stephen King novels, listening as Amy told the customer the price of the book. "Keep the change, love," was his reply, voice rich and slightly accented, as he handed over the money, grabbed up his book and left the shop without another word. Kali heard Amy huff again as the door closed behind the man, the bell ringing softly. "Stuck up, prick," Amy muttered and Kali grinned, though it faded when Amy suddenly snarled. "What the hell is this?!" Turning, she found Amy holding up money that was most certainly not American. "That little thief!" Amy tossed the money on the counter. "That book cost nearly nineteen dollars! My Aunt Carroll's going to freak!" Kali hurried over and looked at the money for a moment before she smiled a bit. "Actually, it's fine." Amy blinked, giving her a very good *Are you shitting me?* expression, before snatching up one of the bills from the counter. "There is no way this," she shook the money at Kali. "Is equivalent to..." "It's British Pounds, Ames." Kali giggled and shook her head, picking up the money and handing it to Amy. "About thirteen pounds to be precise. Which covers the cost of the book and gives about a dollar extra." Amy blinked owlishly, looking at the money she held before stuffing it into the till. "And how do you know all that, Miss Smarty-Pants?" It was Kali' turn to roll her eyes. "I took a business class last semester. We covered foreign money exchange." Amy hummed softly. "Guess he wasn't a prick after all." Kali laughed. "Good to know," she said but saw the odd look on Amy's face as he friend glanced at the door as though she thought the customer was about to walk back in. "Amy?" "Did he seem odd to you?" Kali blinked. "Odd? Odd how?" Amy shrugged. "Just...odd. He seemed pretty tense for a guy just picking up a book." Kali frowned. "I did notice that." Amy nodded, as though Kali had just confirmed some great mystery, before she said, very calmly, very seriously. "He wasn't pack." "What?!" Kali looked at Amy like she'd lost her mind. "Ames...he...he's probably new to town. He..." "He's not pack, Kal." Kali shook her head. "You don't know that." "He smelt like an Alpha who isn't Benjamin." That made Kali blink and her surprise and shock must have been very evident on her face because a low rumble bubbled up from Amy's chest. "You couldn't smell that?" Her friend sounded surprised and a bit suspicious, and Kali merely shrugged, quickly looking away from those sharp blue eyes, instinctively tipping her head to one side and exposing her neck. Sometimes her friend's status as a Beta was a pain. Especially times like this. "Shit," Amy reached out across the counter, managing to awkwardly hug Kali. "I didn't mean...you didn't have to submit..." Kali shrugged again. "Habit," she reasoned before waving her hand to clear the air between them. "As for our...guest...no I did not smell him. Heck, I didn't even think to scent him." Amy studied her silently for a moment before shaking her head. "Ah, well, doesn't matter. He's probably just passing through." "Probably," Kali agreed with a small smile. "Now, how about lunch?" Amy nodded eagerly and led the way back to the break room.

# Chapter Four

Around five that evening Kali told Amy to head home, that she could handle the last hour by herself. Amy, true to fashion, had hesitated before Kali assured it that it was fine, that even if there was a customer or two it wouldn't be as hectic as earlier had been. Not when it was a full moon. Amy still hadn't looked convinced so Kali had resorted to threatening to call Roy and get him to come collect his mate. Amy had huffed and informed her that when she mated then she, Amy, was so going to use that ploy to make Kali do as she said. Kali had laughed and waved her friend off. Now, locking up the shop, Kali sighed and glanced around. Was this what her life was to be? College through the fall and then working in this little book store in the summer? And what about after college? What would she do then? Come back and work in the book store while she had a master's degree in English Literature? Sighing softly, doubling checking the locks and the lights, she grabbed her coat and shoulder bag from the break room before slipping out the back door, locking it behind her. Thankfully the rain had stopped earlier in the afternoon, though the sky remained an ominous grey color. So nature was still threatening rain, it just had yet to open the floodgates. Praying that the weather held long enough for her to get to the meeting circle, Kali climbed onto her bike and headed out.The streets were oddly empty for a Wednesday night, but given that it was a full moon everyone was either heading to, or already at, the meeting circle. The pack ran together during moon nights. Well, everyone but Kali ran together. She was a pack member but hardly considered part of the pack. Too docile, she thought bitterly as she headed down Oak Avenue towards the forest were the meeting circle was set up. Too kind. What kind of she-wolf doesn't have some kind of backbone?She huffed and shook her head.No sense dwelling on things she couldn't change.Once college was done maybe she'd leave.Find another pack.One that would accept her and her peculiarities.If such a pack even existed.As she reached the access road leading into the forest she stopped, leaving her bike against a tree and walking the rest of the way. She could hear and smell the pack. She heard laughter and a small, sad smile graced her face. What wouldn't she give to be included like a normal pack member? What wouldn't she do to have her pack stop looking at her like there was something wrong with her? Like she was a disease that could rub off on them?She continued down the access road until she reached where most of the pack had parked. As she stopped peddling she scented the air, easily finding her parents' scents amid the numerous scents of the pack. She wouldn't end up running with them, she never did, but it was expected that she would at least stand with them during the pack meeting. With a soft sigh she left her bike leaning against the tree before walking the rest of the way to the meeting circle. People glanced at her as she passed, finding her parents by their scent, she walked up beside her mother and stood in silence. Glancing at her mother, Renee, Kali could easily see where both she and her sister got their looks, though Chloe had their father's eyes. Renee Edridge was of average height and was slender, like a jogger or swimmer, with thick, chocolate brown hair and big blue-green eyes. Her skin was pale, like Kali's, but not so much that it made her appear sickly. In Kali's eyes her mother was beautiful. But it was also such a shame that her mother was like everyone else in the pack and thought there was something wrong with Kali. Renee spared Kali a brief look, nodding as though pleased she'd shown up, before returning her focus to the center of the circle where the pack Alpha, Deucalion McRae, was now standing. Swallowing around the sudden lump in her throat, a reaction she'd always had when she saw Deucalion, Kali, like everyone else, bowed her head in respect to Deucalion. "Welcome," Deucalion said as he looked around at the pack, or at those who had thus far gathered. Others would come, later, and join the run on their own. "So, we all know why we're here." He smiled while most of the pack laughed. "Now, as you know there is now a pack in

Lawton which means the forest towards the north has been divided by the council in order to support two packs during the moon. The area has been scent marked so you'll all know where the boundary line is. Please, and this is really for the younger wolves, do not cross the line. Once you are in Lawton territory you will be considered rogue and the Lawton Alpha will deal with you as he sees fit. Understood?" There were murmurs of acknowledging the Alpha's words and Kali knew most would purposely keep the young wolves from the northern section of the woods. Just to prevent anything bad from happening. It made a small smile spread across her face. She'd run the northern section, just to avoid the pack, to avoid being bullied by Chloe and her little flunkies. She drew a deep breath, glancing around and finding Amy standing across the circle, wrapped up in her mate's arms. Her friend looked up at her, a smile gracing her face, and Kali gave a small nod, telling Amy without words that she'd be fine on her own tonight. Amy's eyes showed some concern but then she nodded, turning her head and whispering to Roy, who gaze her a somewhat surprised look before looking over at Kali and giving her a nod. Amy must have asked Roy to let her run with them, thus surprising him by saying it wasn't going to happen. Kali nodded back to him, just to show she understood, before returning her attention to Deucalion, who was leading his Betas, including her father Nolan, off to the woods. The pack broke up then, people heading, in groups, into the trees. Kali watched Amy and Roy disappear through the trees before she turned, picking a random direction, stopping only when a hand touched her arm. Looking over her shoulder she found her mother staring at her."Umm...""I want you to listen to what Alpha Deucalion said about the boundaries," Renee said as Chloe shot Kali a look before walking off with some of her friends."I will.""Kali, it's very important that you watch yourself." Renee gave her a rather serious look. "Getting too close to the boundary line could...well, you could get hurt."Kali found herself in some sort of shock.It was the first time in a long time that her mother had expressed any really concern over her wellbeing. She drew a deep breath and pushed the shock to the back of her mind. "I'll be careful, Mum," she said with a small smile. "You don't need to worry about me."Renee gave her an unreadable look before nodding and walking away, following after Nolan and disappearing into the shadows. Kali sighed softly and shook her head before turning and heading towards the northern part of the forest, she could feel the moon calling to her wolf and the need to run was becoming difficult to ignore.She walked, in human form, for quite a ways until the call to change became too much. Only then did she stop and strip off her clothes, folding them neatly, wrapped in her coat with her shoulder bag, and tucking them beneath some bushes.Stepping back she shivered in the cool night air, gooseflesh breaking out over her skin, head tipping back and her gaze finding the spot in the cloudy sky where the moon hung. With a deep sigh she let the change overtake her, felt her human form slip away like water rushing over rocks and soon she stood as a wolf, glossy white in the darkness of the forest. Shaking herself to remove the last tingles of the change she threw her head back and howled.

# Chapter Five

There was nothing in the world that felt as freeing to Kali as when she ran in her wolf form. The wind over her fur. The earth beneath her paws. The scents and sounds all amplified The world became different all while staying the same. Leaping over a fallen log she yipped happily, running faster and faster. She pushed herself until her muscles ached and even then she kept running. This was freedom. True freedom. Better than any of her favourite books. Better than hot chocolate on a cold winter day. Better, even, than the dream of leaving her pack to find one that was more accepting of her nature. Dashing through the underbrush she caught the scent of a nearby rabbit. Turning on a dime, she easily located the little creature, not surprised when it bolted. She yipped and gave chase. She didn't intend to harm it. She might be a wolf but she wasn't that much of a predator. When she got close enough to the rabbit she bumped it with her nose before letting it run off. A laugh bubbled up from her chest, though in wolf form it was more of a chuffing sound, before she slowed her pace, coming easily to a stop. Panting for breath she looked around to get her bearings. She was in the northern part of the forest. She could hear CherokeeFalls and see the rock terrain that led up to the foot of the mountains. Lifting her head, muzzle pointing towards the sky, she scented the air, searching for signs of other wolves. Pack and otherwise. When she found nothing, just the faintest marking scent, she knew she was still a good distance from the boundary line. Taking a moment to stretch, letting her muscles settle back into place after her brisk run, she turned and walked through the forest towards the waterfall. She'd get a quick drink and then take another run before circling back to this area. If she stayed in and around this area she would be just fine. It was far enough north that none of the pack would come looking for her but not so far as to run the risk of crossing the boundary line into Lawton Pack territory. Reaching the stream she scented the air again, though with the rushing water it was nearly impossible to tell who or what was nearby, though she managed to determine that she was alone. With a soft huff she bent her head and began lapping at the cool water, ears twitching slightly, listening for any sort of movement. She might have felt safe, and there might be a good chance that no one else would venture this far north, but when it came to her sister things were never completely certain. Chloe had proven before just how far she would push the line if it meant humiliating Kali. Once her thirst was quenched and her muscles no longer screamed in protest at the simplest movement, Kali turned away from the water, about to head off for another run, only to go still as stone when a twig snapped a few feet in front of her. Fear crawled down her spine. Had Chloe followed her? Was she about to experience yet another public humiliation? She wanted to run, to avoid any sort of confrontation with her sister and her flunky friends, but her fear kept her rooted to the spot, watching as the bushes rustled and then parted. Her heart leapt into her throat and the blood in her veins ran cold as ice. The wolf that stepped from the underbrush was most certainly not her sister. Nor was it any member of her pack. The wolf, a male, was massive. Bigger even than Deucalion. With thick fur the color of a starless night sky. A low growl bubbled up from the male as he drew himself to full height, making himself even larger, his tail lifting and hackles peeling back in a display of dominance that was completely unmistakable. And even if it had been, she could feel his rank even from the distance that separating them. Alpha, her mind whispered, the fear now accompanied by the instinct to submit. But this was not Deucalion. This was not her Alpha. She forced herself to move, to lower herself just enough to show submission, hoping it might buy her time, stepping back carefully at the same time. What on earth was an Alpha doing on Henson Pack territory? It didn't make any sense. She'd smelled the boundary line. And it...her heart leapt again, pounding against her ribs. The boundary line was behind her. It had to be. She must have passed it while running and not even realized. Which meant the strange Alpha was not on Henson Pack territory. She was in territory belonging to the Lawton Pack. She made a soft sound and started to slowly step back, keeping her tail tucked to her belly and ears flattened in signs of submission, silently praying the Alpha showed mercy and let her leave as a warning to the others of her pack. She froze again, however, when a second wolf, also a male, emerged from the bushes. Not as large as the Alpha, more lean and shaggy, with grey fur splotched with brown. She watched the newcomer stepped up beside the Alpha, standing at the black wolf's shoulder. The newcomer's position was lowered but not like Kali's was. The grey-brown wolf was a Beta. And from the looks of it a Lead Beta. Second only to the Alpha. Not good, she thought frantically while trying to figure out how to get away from the two. If she could run, make it back over the boundary line, she would be safe. Hopefully. The Lawton Alpha wouldn't give chase if she entered her own pack territory. He'd let her go. Though the odds of actually getting away were now slim. Oh, this is so not good! When the Beta looked at his Alpha, the large black wolf huffed, teeth still barred and then snarled. His intent was clear. The Beta started to look at her, body tense and ready for a fight, and that was all the warning she needed. With a low whine she bolted to her right. She heard the Beta snarl and the Alpha howl and silently prayed the massive wolf wasn't calling for reinforcements. One or two wolves she might be able to outrun but if the pack, or even a small group of Betas, showed up she was done. They'd kill her as a rogue. And that was if the Alpha and Lead Beta, who were chasing after her, didn't get to her first. She ran with all her might, pushing her body to its limits, all while listening as the wolves behind managed to keep pace with her, though they didn't seem able to over take her. She might just have a chance after all. Provided that she could stay ahead of them.Darting through the trees and underbrush, Kali did her best to lose the Alpha and Beta, all while attempting to double back in order to get across the boundary line. She was running out of time. She had to do something. Had to get more distance between her and her pursuers. Leaping over a fallen tree she glanced around quickly, trying to gauge which direction would be best. She had just dashed around a massive oak when the leaves and dead plant life beneath her paws unexpectedly shifted, revealing a steep incline in which she was now perched precariously at the top of.Her balance went out the window the moment the ground beneath her paws was no longer somewhat even. She yelped as she was pitched sideways, rolling down the hill like a doll tossed from a child's hand. Reaching the bottom she landed on her side, effectively knocking the wind out of herself. She whined loudly with what little air was left in her lungs and tried to scramble to her feet, survival instinct pushing her to get up, to keep running. Not just lay there like a defeated dog.But by the time she managed to draw a lungful of air it was too late.The Beta was on her. Literally.Despite being smaller than his Alpha, the Beta was still much larger than she was, and he easily pinned her beneath his bulk, jaws closing firmly around the scruff of her neck, ready to kill her at his Alpha's command.The Alpha, Kali quickly discovered, had easily made his way down the incline and was now standing, staring down at her. She whined softly, body going lax beneath the Beta, everything in her submitting immediately in the hopes that the Lawton Alpha might show mercy and allow her to live. She looked up at him, eyes pleading and fearful, only to go as ridged as a board when her gaze met with the ice blue eyes of the black wolf. She was suddenly warm, much warmer than she should be and it had nothing to do with the Beta pinning her. A tingling sensation spread throughout her entire body and something, some little cog in her mind and soul, suddenly seemed to click into place. She could tell the Alpha felt something similar because he suddenly stopped growling and his eyes, which reminded her of a frozen tundra under a full moon, filled with surprise.She made another low sound, something between a whine and a purr, all while her tail softly thumped the ground. Her gaze never leaving the Alpha's face. A single word filtered through the haze of happiness that had descended into her mind. A single word that held more weight and power than any other.Mate.

# Chapter Six

The Alpha made a low sound and stopped forward, causing the Beta to release her and step away, whining faintly as though confused by his Alpha's sudden change of heart. Kali's tail continued to wag as she lifted her head, exposing her throat to her mate on instinct, whimpering quietly as the Alpha's head lower, his nose pressing into the fur of her neck. He sniffed her for a moment before he rumbled loudly, throwing his head back and howling. She hesitated for a moment, uncertain what to do when he looked down at her, but she slowly rose up a bit, licking at the Alpha, at her mate's, muzzle. He rumbled again and suddenly stepped away. She whined and watched him, trying to understand what he was doing. Was this some kind of rejection? If so why had he even scented her? Why accept her submission? She whined again just as the Beta stepped into her line of sight. Instinct had her gaze snapping to his face, trying to gauge what he was planning to do, meeting warm brown eyes without flinching. She made a low sound, something that if she had been human would have been a gasp of surprise, as the warmth that she'd felt when realizing the Alpha was her mate intensified. Her entire body was tingling even stronger than before and she quickly realized why the Alpha had stepped away like he had. Two mates, she thought as the Beta's tail suddenly began wagging, his eyes lighting up with joy. I've got two mates. The Beta bounced towards her then, and though she flinched back slightly, the adrenaline and instinct guiding her movements, he didn't seem to notice, he buried his nose into the fur of her neck and inhaled, scenting her deeply all while his tail continued to wag and he made happy little huffing noises. She made a soft sound, lifting her head to scent him back and ended up yelping in surprise when he leapt, tackling her playfully and rolling them through the leaves. She couldn't help but nip playfully at him as they tumbled. All her life she'd dreamt of finding her mate. And now she had. Her mind was still reeling with the knowledge that she had two and that they were both so accepting of her. She certainly hadn't expected that. Would it change though, when they learned that she wasn't a fierce, wild she-wolf? Would they still want her? She yelped again when, just as she pinned her Beta mate to the ground, his tongue lolling from one side of his mouth, her Alpha mate was against her side, pushing her, gently, off to the side before he began rubbing along her side. It took a minute for her to realize what he was doing. Scent marking. Declaring her as his before they ever completed the mating. A sudden jolt went through her at the thought of being properly claimed by her mates. And just how would that work? Were they mates with each other as well? Or would they have to share her?Before she could ponder that train of thought any further her Beta mate leapt forward, pressing against her, scent marking her, all while nipping at the Alpha's ear.She pushed back against the her Beta, making happy sounds as she scent marked him, before turning her attention to her Alpha, rubbing her face along his shoulder. She heard him rumble, heard the joy in that sound, and she wagged her tail excitedly as she scent marked him, laying claim to him as he and her Beta laid claim to her.After a few minutes the Alpha rumbled again, stepping away from her and Beta, loping a few steps away, pausing long enough to look back at them and let out a soft bark. Her Beta bumped her shoulder before following the Alpha. She huffed happily and trotted after them. The Alpha gave her muzzle a quick lick before he broke immediately into a run, the Beta barking happily before chasing after him. She watched them for a moment before she let out a huff and ran after them, easily catching up to them before using a sudden burst of speed to overtake them.She heard the Alpha howl, this time it was a happy sound, a sound that was playful, and suddenly he was at her shoulder, though it was obvious he was pushing himself to keep up with her. The Beta yowled from behind them, clearly not liking that he was being left behind. After a little while she slowed, letting her Alpha take the lead, dropping back to run beside her Beta, who bumped her, nipping gently at her shoulder as they followed the Alpha into a hunt, the clear scent of a deer filling their noses.Kali scented the air with each step, even though her Alpha was leading them directly to the deer, her Beta huffed as he moved, running easily to the left, planning to flank the deer once they found it. He and the Alpha had clearly hunted before. That left her feeling a bit out of place as she didn't know what she was supposed to do, so she merely followed the Alpha's lead.A short time later and they came upon the deer, standing amongst a few pine trees, grazing peacefully until its head snapped up, ears twitching as its eyes searched the darkness of the forest. Its nostrils flared and, just as it caught their scents, it bolted, leaping over a fallen tree and heading for the deeper part of the forest.Her Alpha growled and together they all ran harder, faster, her Beta breaking away and heading for higher ground while she and her Alpha chased the deer towards the creek. The were closing on it within no time but before she could leap, before she could attempt to make the kill, her Beta leapt down from an out jut of rocks, jaws closing firmly around the deer's throat, dragging it down as he dropped, paws finding the ground quickly. The deer struggled but the Alpha quickly leapt up and grabbed the deer by the back of the neck, his fangs sinking deep even as he shook his head, attempting to break the neck even as the Beta used his hold to crush the windpipe.Kali skidded to a halt, watching her mates bring the deer down with a deep, instinctual sense of pride. It was an old instinct, as old as her species, that she-wolves had developed. It was meant to tell a she-wolf that her mate, or in Kali's case mates, could provide not only for her but for the pups they would one day have. Even though the instinct was old and basically outdated, Kali couldn't help the swell of pride she felt as she watched her mates release the now dead deer. Her Beta licked his muzzle, smearing the blood through his fur, before he turned to her, tail wagging. She stepped towards him, licking at his muzzle, showing her appreciation for what he'd done. After a moment she turned, intending to do the same to her Alpha but he stepped closer to her, bumping shoulders before he nodded towards the deer. It took a moment for her to realize just what her Alpha was doing but when it hit her she was shocked enough that if she had been in human form she might very well have fainted. He was an Alpha and he was offering her the chance to eat first. Mate or not it spoke of how dedicated he already was to their mating even though they hadn't claimed each other yet. Alphas, even many who were mated, never let anyone eat before them. It was as much to do with pack standing as with possessive instincts. She made a happy sound, licking his muzzle before moving to the deer, eating her fill before she stepped back and went to lay a few feet away, watching as her Alpha and Beta ate together. It was another surprise but perhaps the two were close enough that the Alpha felt comfortable enough to allow his Lead Beta to eat with him. It made her hopeful that their mating wouldn't be as tense as she'd first thought, especially if the two males were not mated to each other as well as her. Resting her head on her paws she closed her eyes and listened to the soft sounds of the forest, barely twitching when her mates were suddenly laying to either side of her, one licking the blood and bits of meat from her muzzle while the other groomed the fur at the back of her neck. For the first time in her life she felt content. She felt accepted.

## chapter seven

Kali woke with sunlight streaming across her face. She murmured softly, turning her head into the pillow, drawing a deep breath as she tried to fight off waking. She was comfortable, completely relaxed, and wasn't ready to get up and face the world. With her face pressed into the pillow she easily drew in the scents that lingered there. Scents that had her smiling even as she rubbed her face into the pillow, drawing more and more of the scents, her mates scents, into her lungs. She could still remember leaving the forest with them last night, could remember following them to a massive house at the edge of the town of Lawton. What happened after they'd gotten to the house made her cheeks burn and an ache to immediately form between her legs. She reached up and touched her shoulder, fingertips sliding lightly over the mating mark her Alpha mate had placed there during their claiming the previous night. On the opposite side of her neck was a second mark. Her Beta mate's mark. Unlike other marks or wounds these marks would never go away. They were permenant. They would show any wolf who saw them that she was mated.It was rare to have two mates, she could only think of a handful of times when she'd heard of it, but after last night, after the claiming her mates had gifted her with, she was glad of having two. She felt privileged that fate had deemed her worthy of two mates. Especially mates who were an Alpha and a Beta of their own pack.That thought caused her heart to skip a bit.She was mated. Claimed.She would have to leave her old pack.That thought alone was enough to sap some of her happiness and replace it with fear and nervousness.Was she ready for that step? Was she ready to leave her old life behind in favour of a new one?Drawing a deep breath she decided that, at that moment, it didn't matter. She could figure that out later. Right now she wanted her mates. Lifting her head from the pillow she glanced around her. The bed, large enough for at least four people, was empty save for her, though the sheets were still fairly warm, meaning that her mates hadn't been gone for very long. Still smiling she looked around the room. It was large, spacious and tastefully furnished. It had a very homey feel and it warmed her to know that at least one of her mates was down to earth.Slowly climbing from the bed she looked around for her clothes, no way was she walking around naked even if it was her mate's home, only to remember that her clothes were still out in the forest. Folded neatly right where she'd left them, and her shoulder bag, back in her old pack's territory. With a soft sigh she looked around, spotting a shirt draped over the arm of the desk chair in the corner. Grabbing it up she easily identified her Alpha mate's scent and her smile widened as she held the fabric to her nose, inhaling deeply, the soft cotton of the shirt rubbing gently against her face. After a moment she slipped the shirt on. It was far too big for her, pooling around her body more like a blanket than a shirt, and she wasn't surprised to find the hem reached almost to her knees. She started to reach for the buttons only to be forced to stop and roll the sleeves up passed her elbows first. Once she was clothed, or rather as clothed as possible, she headed towards the door, pausing only long enough to listen for any movement in the hallway. Satisfied that she was in no immediate danger she opened the door and stepped out in the hallway. Scenting the air her stomach growled as she caught the scent of bacon and eggs cooking. Following her nose she eventually ended up in the kitchen doorway. A man, tall with dark hair, stood at the stove, his back to her. Instinctively she scented the air, but with the cooking food it was impossible to catch the man's scent. She fidgeted nervously, debating the risks of speaking, when arms suddenly wrapped around her waist making her jump and a soft cry of surprise fall from her lips, causing the man at the stove to whirl around. She was focused, however, on the man behind her. His scent tickling her nose and she immediately recognized the scent of her Beta mate. Turning her head she looked at him, smiling softly as the while, taking in his happy expression and rich, chocolate coloured eyes. Kay, she remembered his name being Kay. Kay Yorke. She remembered her surprise when she'd first seen him in human form. Recognizing him as the man who'd been in the book store yesterday. The man that had unnerved Amy so much. She couldn't help but wonder what her best friend's reaction would be to learn that he had turned out to be one of her mates. "Hello, darling," he purred in her ear, nuzzling her hair affectionately. "Hi," she whispered, suddenly feeling very shy, even though this man was her mate. He smiled at her. "Hope you're hungry, darling," he said as he looked at the man by the stove. "Thornton's cooked enough food for an army." She heard a snort and looked at the man by the stove, recognizing him immediately as her other mate. The Lawton Pack Alpha, Thornton Garroway. He smiled at her when he noticed her looking at him, those vibrant blue eyes shining brightly. "Did you sleep well, love?" She nodded. "I did," she said as Kay's hand splayed over her abdomen, rubbing lightly while he nuzzled the mark he had left on her neck, making her giggle as his curly hair brushed faintly over her skin. "Kay, that tickles." She felt him grin against her neck and she whimpered softly as he kissed and nipped at his mark. Shivering against him she couldn't help but lean back, resting her body against him, head tipping to the side, giving him more room. She felt, rather than heard, Kay's rumble of appreciation and she suspected they were about to head back to the bedroom when Thornton cleared his throat. "Kay, don't molest Kali until after breakfast please." Kali couldn't help but giggle as Kay lifted his head, letting his chin rest on her shoulder and he gave Thornton a pouty look. "You used to be fun," he said as he rubbed Kali's abdomen through her shirt. "And it's not molesting when she's our mate." "Be that as it may, our mate hasn't eaten since some time yesterday and after last night I'm certain she is more hungry than horny at the moment," Thornton retorted, accent drifting through the air and making Kali shiver with want. Oh now that's just unfair, she thought as she watched him turn the stove off and carry plates of food to the table. He could say the silliest thing ever and I would probably still turn into a puddle of goo. "Well maybe she should be allowed to decide what she wants to do," Kay fired back, kissing Kali's cheek which made her smile. "So, Kali my dear, what do you want, hmm? You want to eat or do you want to..." Before Kay could finish what he was saying Kali's stomach growled, loudly, and her cheeks turned red in embarrassment.

# Chapter Eight

"I...I..." Kali felt her face heat up even more, the blush spreading from her cheeks to her entire face. "It's alright, love," Thornton was quick to reassure her as he walked over, reaching up to brush her hair back from her face, his hand lingering to cup her cheek, smiling the entire time. "After the full moon and our...well...rigorous activities last night it's understandable that you're hungry." Kali's blush intensified and she made a soft whimpering sound before burying her face in Thornton's neck, trying to hide her embarrassment. She felt Kay trying to keep from laughing and couldn't resist the urge to nudge him with her elbow. He grunted dramatically and then whimpered as though she had actually hurt him, when he nuzzled her neck it made her giggle against Thornton's neck. "So," Kali said after lifting her head, peering up at Thornton through her lashes, trying to pretend that Kay wasn't still nuzzling her neck suggestively. "Breakfast?" Thornton chuckled and nodded, thumb rubbing over her cheek for a moment before he took her hand, Kay releasing her instantly, and walked her to the table. She wasn't surprised that, after she had taken a seat, Kay dropped, not so gracefully, into the chair next to her grinning like a little boy who just got away with stealing cookies before dinner. She giggled while Thornton rolled his eyes, taking a seat across the table from them. As they ate they talked, asking questions and learning a little bit about one another. Kali chuckled at a story Kay told about Thornton when they were young and had just reached for another piece of toast when someone, a Lawton Pack member, came bursting into the kitchen. She jerked in surprise and reflexively sank back in her chair, instincts screaming that she wasn't pack. She was an outsider and this man would likely tear her throat out. Even Kay's hand on her arm didn't calm the sudden pounding of her heart as she kept her eyes fixed on the newcomer even as Thornton stood, placing himself instinctively between his pack member and her. "Alpha..." The man, tall with sandy brown hair and milky green eyes stopped, eyes fixing on her and surprise was written clear as day on his face. "Who..." Kay growled unexpectedly, stopping only when Thornton gave him a warning look. Kali shook in her chair, reaching out and grabbing hold of Kay's hand, lacing their fingers together and trying to use the connection to calm down. Her mates wouldn't let anything happen to her. "Andrew," Thornton said the name firmly, with every bit of authority of an Alpha, and the man's eyes immediately left Kali, his focus completely on his Alpha.

"What was it that you needed?" "It's..." Andrew glanced briefly at Kali again, clearly wanting to ask who she was but not wanting to risk his Alpha's anger. "It's Samson. He's..." "Say no more. Where is he?" "The bar down on Haven Street." With a nod Thornton turned, looking at Kay. "I'll handle this," he said and Kay nodded his understanding. "Why don't you and Kali spend the morning together? I'll be back as soon as I can." Thornton gave Kali a warm smile before he and Andrew left. S waited a moment before turning to Kay. "Who's Samson?" "A nuisance." Kay didn't sound like he was overly thrilled with Thornton going off without him and Kali gave his hand a squeeze, trying to distract him, which worked, at least a little, since he leaned over and nuzzled her cheek. He sighed softly, kissing her cheek as he pulled back a bit, smiling just a little. "Samson's just...he's a pain in the ass," he said after a moment, rubbing his thumb over the back of her hand. "I honestly don't know why Thornton even keeps him around. He's a useless drunk who always picks fights and starts trouble." "Every pack as someone like that," she said softly, thinking of Donald McGullan, an elderly man from her pack who was a lot like the man Kay described. "But they're still pack. You can't just go tossing them out because they're not like everyone else." Kay chuckled and gave her this curious little look. "What?" "It's nothing," he said, still chuckling a bit. "Well it's just...Thornton says pretty much the same thing. And, honestly, when Samson's off the bottle for a good stretch he's a perfectly fine Gamma. He just...needs to get his shit straightened out I suppose. Thornton's patience isn't limitless." "Do you really think Thornton would force this man from the pack?" Kay shrugged. "If he was left with no other option. The pack is only as strong as its individual members. And Samson's...problem...doesn't just affect him." "Maybe he just needs someone to help him." Kay's head tipped to one side a bit, his eyes never leaving her face, silently studying her in a way that she was unfamiliar with. It had just started to bother her when he smiled, leaning over to nuzzle her neck affectionately. "You're amazing, darling, do you know that?" Kali blinked. "For what? Suggesting the obvious?" He grinned. "Not every wolf would think about Samson needing help. They'd either force him out of the pack or kill him." Kali's nose wrinkled in distaste but before she could say anything Kay kissed her cheek. "You're amazingly wonderful." She felt the blush bloom in her cheeks and quickly ducked her head, trying to hide it. She wasn't used to being complimented. Hell, she wasn't used to being treated the way Kay was treating her. It was a lot to take in. Especially given the short amount of time she had known her mate. She smiled as she looked at him, seeing the joy written clear as day on his face, she decided that this was a life she could get used to.

# Chapter Nine

A short while later found Kali dozing on the couch with Kay. They'd spent the time talking, getting to know one another a little bit better. She learned that Kay had been born to a pack in Ireland but at the tender age of sixteen he met Thornton who had mated him shortly after and he'd moved to a little town just north of London to be with the Alpha. She also learned the reason for the Lawton Pack's sudden upheaval and relocation from the United Kingdom to America. Hunters. Humans who knew about their kind and had decided, centuries ago, that they were abominations that needed to be eradicated like vermin. Listening to Kay explain about how the attack, so sudden and unexpected, had wiped out nearly half the pack, Kali had hugged him tightly and nuzzled his neck comfortingly, all while tears burned her eyes. She could have easily lost him, lost Thornton, before ever finding them. All because a group of humans thought they shouldn't exist. She hugged him even now, not wanting to let go almost as though she was afraid if she let go he would disappear. Sensing her upset, Kay had kissed her temple and nuzzled her hair, hugging her close and telling her that it was okay. That the Hunters couldn't possibly track them here, the Council had made certain of it, and that everything would be alright. It had helped a little but she couldn't help worry. Hunters were not known for giving up easily. Especially not when wolves had escaped their grasp. But Kay was right. The odds of the pack being found again were slim. Especially if the Council had taken precautions. Kay must have known the topic of conversation bothered her because he quickly asked about her. About her life. There wasn't much to tell. She explained about growing up in Henson, leaving out how her entire pack, save for a few, treated her like an outsider. She talked about college, about the degree she was studying for and working at the bookshop. She talked about Amy, and the trouble they got up to when they'd been little, laughing with him the whole while. When he asked how she felt about leaving home, leaving her old pack, she just shrugged and said it would be okay. That she found her mates and that that was what mattered. Now they were snuggled together, Kay laying on his back with Kali sprawled over him, her head cushioned on his chest with one of his hands resting on her back while the other played with her hair. She smiled and rubbed her cheek against his chest as she closed her eyes, reaching up to toy with some of his curls, wrapping them lightly, gently, around her fingers, making him smile even as his eyes slipped shut. She listened to the sound of his heartbeat, listened to the steady, gentle rhythm and let everything sink in. Truly sink in. If she was truly honest with herself she was a little afraid. A new chapter of her life was unfolding and she had no idea what was going to happen. She also had no idea how her family, how her pack, was going to react to the news of her mating. Would they be happy? Would they even care? It was enough to give her a headache just worrying about it. She opened her eyes and glanced across the room at the clock. Nearly noon now. Had anyone noticed her absence? Had her parents begun to worry yet? Sighing softly she decided that right now it didn't matter. She'd deal with all of that when she had to. Turning her head a bit she stretched upwards and pressed a soft kiss to Kay's jaw, his stubble scratchy and odd against her lips, but she found she rather liked it. It was nice and the faint dusting of dark stubble suited her Beta. Made him look rugged and handsome. Though she suspected that he would be just as handsome clean shaven. When he unexpectedly tipped his head, kissing her lips all without opening his eyes she let out a startled squeak, which made his smile widen as his eyes opened just a tiny bit. "You're so pretty when you blush," he whispered, reaching up to cup her cheek, his thumb brushing over the skin just below her eye, and she felt her cheeks heat up even more, the blush spreading. "Fucking gorgeous." "She is, isn't she?" Kali startled at the voice, even though she immediately recognized it as Thornton's. She felt Kay's arms tighten around her, the hand still on her back rubbed calming circles. "I'm sorry, love," Thornton said as Kali looked towards him, finding him standing just a few feet away. "I didn't mean to scare you." "You...You didn't..." Kali shook her head as Thornton walked over, kneeling beside the couch, hand lifting to run through her hair. "It's alright, love," he all but cooed, leaning in to nuzzle at her neck, pressing kisses as soft as a butterfly's wing over the skin. She made a soft sound, relaxing and trying to press closer to Thornton without abandoning her place atop Kay. She heard her Beta mate chuckle, his hands sliding to her hips to steady her, all while Thornton moved, climbing up on the couch behind her, straddling Kay's legs. Kali turned her head the moment Thornton's hands curled around her sides, fingers spread wide over her ribs, pushing back against his chest, instinctively seeking contact with her mate. When he kissed her cheek she whined softly, a demanding sound even though she wasn't really certain what she was demanding. Thankfully Thornton seemed to know because he pressed another kiss to her cheek before claiming her lips in a passionate, dominating kiss. She was panting heavily when they broke apart, the world around her narrowing down to nothing but her and her mates. She whined again, another demanding sound, Kay's hands tightened in response and Thornton rumbled, nuzzling at her neck again. "I suggest," the Alpha rumbled, his words deep and his accent thick, making Kali shiver and press closer to him. "That we take this to the bedroom." "An excellent idea," Kay responded as one of his hands glided up from Kali's hips to rest over Thornton's. Kali could somehow feel the heat of both and she squirmed with want. "What do you say, mate?" Kali couldn't seem to find her words but she did nod vigorously, which made Kay grin and Thornton chuckle. The next thing she knew Thornton was standing and swinging her up into his arms. She let out a surprised cry, arms flying around his neck as he carried her, bridal style, towards the stairs. Pressing her face into his neck she heard Kay laughing as he followed after them. Bad, bad mates, she thought before nipping playfully at Thornton's neck, enjoying the way he groaned and held her closer. She smiled and decided that, right now, she'd worry about her family and whatever their issues over her mating might be later. Right now was about her and her mates.

## Chapter Ten

It had been two weeks since her mating and Kali hadn't managed to find the courage to tell her parents that she was mated. Every time she thought she was ready something in her froze and the words turned to ash in her mouth. It was ridiculous. This was supposed to be a joyous thing and she felt wretched because she didn't think her family would care. They'd shown little concern over her comings and goings over the last few weeks, all the times she'd snuck off so she could visit her mates, so why would they show anything more if she told them she was mated? Was she really that afraid of their reaction? Or was she just afraid of the change it would mean? She'd have to leave the only home she'd ever known. Leave her only friend. Leave everything to start over again with Thornton and Kay. Drawing a deep breath she paused along the path leading from the forest to Thornton's house. She knew her mates were waiting, were getting frustrated more and more every day that she didn't tell her family about their mating. Kay did a better job of hiding it than Thornton did but she still saw it, saw the sadness starting to fill his eyes whenever she told them she hadn't told her family. She hated that she was putting that look in his eyes. Hated that she was causing her mate any sort of pain. But it was Thornton that had her truly worried. The last few times she'd been to the house she'd seen the anger in his eyes. He was growing impatient with her. Growing tired of her excuses. She knew it would only be a matter of time before he finally had enough. She just had no idea what she was going to do when that happened. With another deep breath she headed for the house, letting herself in the back door which led to the kitchen. She was just about to call out to announce her presence when Thornton and Kay both came in from the hallway. "Hey," she said with a smile until she noticed the rather icy look on Kay's face and the infuriated one on Thornton's. "Umm..." "Did you tell your parents about us yet," Thornton demanded, crossing his arms and giving her a look that could have frozen water. "Umm..." She shuffled her feet nervously, tugging at the strap of her shoulder bag. "Well..." She saw the disappointment in Kay's eyes and Thornton growled. "Why? What's more important than announcing our mating?" "Nothing!" Kali shook her head. "Nothing is! I just...I'm not...I..." "You're just stringing us along is what you're doing!" Kali flinched at the harshness of Thornton's words, her instincts screaming that she had to submit, had to pacify the Alpha, but the mating instinct refused to let her.

Thornton wasn't her Alpha, he was her mate and she didn't have to submit. Not now and not every. That didn't mean she wasn't afraid of what he might do given how angry he was right now. "I'm not stringing you along! I'm not!" "Then you can fucking explain this," Thornton sneered and tossed a bunch of photos onto the table. Kali flinched at his words, and the venom in his tone, as if he'd hit her. She picked up a few of the photos, looking through them before looking back up at him. She felt a shock of surprise shoot through her followed by confusion, disbelief and a hint of anger. "Is this...have you been following me?" "One of my Gammas happened to be at the market and saw you. She was going to stop and speak to you but stopped when she saw that." Kali's hands began shaking as she looked down at the photos again. It was a few days ago at the Barrington Market. She'd gone with Amy and Roy and while Amy had been off getting some organic carrots Roy had told her that he and Amy were expecting their first baby. She'd been so excited, so happy for them, that she'd practically jumped him, hugging him and laughing as she congratulated them. The photos she held showed all of it but looked more like she was being unfaithful to her mates. Like she was throwing herself into the arms of another man. "Thornton..." "We're your mates," Thornton snapped, cutting her off and causing her gaze to immediately shoot to his face. "How could you lie to us like this?" "Lie?" Kali shook her head, throwing the photos back on the table. "How did I lie?" "You said you weren't ready to tell your family about our mating when instead you were running around with another man!" Thornton roared and took a menacing step forward, hands balled into fists at his side, and Kali felt herself start to shake. As quickly as she could she moved, putting the table between them which made Thornton sneer at her. "You cower in fear because you know you deserve our anger!" "I should never be afraid of you no matter what I've done," Kali whispered in a shaky voice. "Those photos aren't proof of anything..." "Our Gamma said she saw him drag you off behind a building where the two of you fucked." Kali looked at Kay with wide eyes. It was the first time he'd spoken since this had started but his words cut deeper than any knife. "Is that what you think?" "She said you seemed to enjoy yourself quite a bit," Thornton snarled with complete contempt. "And you believed her, just like that," Kali whispered as sorrow filled her, all her dreams of being with her mates in any sort of happy, loving relationship shattered like glass. "You didn't think to ask if there's another explanation or want to hear my side of it, you just believed her." "Is there another explanation," Kay asked quickly, hopefully, ignoring the sharp glare Thornton sent his way. "Yes, but if you think I'm going to give it to you, you can go screw yourselves." The hope that had been in Kay's eyes quickly diminished and he made a low sound, looking like he wanted to move, to reach for her, but he stayed where he was. Thornton huffed angrily and drew her attention back to her Alpha mate. "You're not going to deny you fucked that guy? Not going to deny you betrayed us?" Thornton asked, and Kali could tell he would never believe there was any other explanation if she begged and pleaded with them until she was blue in the face."You don't deserve for me to waste my time when we both know you won't believe me," she replied as tears filled her eyes but she blinked them away, refusing to cry in front of them. Not now. Not ever. "Why should we believe you," Thornton growled, completely missing the tears and hurt in her eyes. "We've got proof right there and our Gamma's testimony. You've probably never wanted to really be our mate. Too happy playing the field and screwing God knows how many of the men in your pack."He looked like he thought he'd won something with that comment, thought he'd gotten everything right. If he only knew the damage he'd done with it instead."Go to hell," Kali whispered and went out the back door. The tears fell freely the second she was outside and she had to choke back a sob. She walked a short distant from the house, until her emotions started to threaten to overtake her and then she broke into a run, heading straight for the forest.She ran blindly, barely noticing her surroundings, her instincts guiding her through Lawton land until she'd crossed the pack boundary. Even when she was back in Henson Pack territory she kept running. She ran until nature seemed to decide she needed to stop. Her foot caught a tree root and she went crashing to the ground, crying out when she landed on her right arm the wrong way and her cheek scraped against the tree.She sobbed as she lay there, unable to find the strength to get up. Unable to ignore the sorrow and the pain that was tearing her heart apart. She felt like she was drowning and there was nothing she could do about it. So she just lay there and let it drag her down into a darkness she wasn't sure she wanted to find a way out of.

# Chapter Eleven

Kali woke slowly, coming up from the darkness like floating to the surface of the lake after diving in. Her eyes fluttered open and she found herself staring at the crushed and fallen leaves and twigs that littered the forest floor. Darkness had settled over the forest, meaning she'd been out for quite some time and yet she didn't seem to care. Her world had just shattered into tiny pieces. Why should it matter that she'd been in the forest for hours? Why should it matter that no one had probably noticed her absence? Why should anything ever matter again when her mates had just cast her aside like she meant nothing to them? A low sound, something like a pain filled whine, bubbled up from her chest and she immediately curled into a ball, ignoring the pain in her leg and cheek as tears filled her eyes, sliding silently down her face, dripping to the soil below her and disappearing as though they'd never been in the first place. She squeezed her eyes shut and tried to forget the way Thornton and

Kay had looked at her. The rage and disappointment. Nothing hurt worse than that. Knowing her mates didn't trust her. That they saw her as someone capable of betraying the most sacred bond their kind had.Another of those pain filled whines left her and she curled in a tighter ball, the floodgates threatening to burst, hands clenching, fingers digging into the dirt as she fought to push the pain, the grief and the heartbreak, into some corner of her mind where it wouldn't effect her anymore. She wanted to just not feel it. She wanted to be like ice and feel nothing.She bit her lip as another whine started to bubble up, fighting to force it back down. She wouldn't give them that too. She'd already given them her tears. Even if they hadn't seen it. She wouldn't give them anything more. She wouldn't!She was so lost to her emotions, to trying to become cold and unfeeling, that she didn't notice she wasn't alone until she heard a twig snap. She reacted instantly, pushing up as quickly as she could, sitting in the leaves and dirt and looking in the direction the snapping twig was. She stilled instantly when she caught sight of a lanky wolf standing just a foot or two from her.The wolf, male and from the scent of it a Gamma, was small for its rank. The smoky grey and black fur matted and dingy, obviously in need of a good grooming, its eyes were a pale blue, like the fading afternoon sky. It didn't approach her, just stood and watched, body relaxed and at ease.She drew a deep breath, catching the wolf's scent and she frowned, reaching up to wipe the tears that still clung to her cheeks, dotted her lashes, away with a quick brush of her fingers. She knew that scent. Had only smelled it two or three times but she knew it."Samson?"She watched as the wolf shifted, fur and claws sliding away to reveal the human beneath.Samson Crowe, Gamma of the Lawton Pack, crouched a few feet from her, watching her.She'd met him, when Thornton and Kay had first introduced her to the pack as their mate. She had remembered how Kay had told her that Samson was a drunk and problem for the pack. She hadn't seen the man as such. She'd seen a man, beaten down and broken by the world, and she had felt sorry for him. Felt sorry that no one had taken the time to see the real him. To see the pain and hurt and grief in those haunted eyes.Even now, in the darkness of the forest, she could still see the pain in those eyes.What she didn't understand was what he was doing here. He was on Henson Pack territory. If he was found Deucalion would kill him as a trespasser. Her mates might think Samson wasn't worth fighting for or protecting but she wasn't going to let the man be hurt just because he'd stumbled a little far from home."Samson...you...you can't be here." She moved then, ignoring the still throbbing pain in her ankle and cheek, scooting towards him. "My...The pack...they'll...""I saw you run from Thornton's house," Samson said softly, his voice gruff but kind, and it was then that Kali couldn't ever remember the man having spoken so much the few times she been around him. "You were crying. And...well...those two buggers might not have cared enough to make sure you were alright but I just...I..."Kali felt more tears pool in her eyes and she quickly blinked them away. "You wanted to make sure I was okay." He gave a small nod and she resisted the urge to just bawl. This man wasn't family or her mate and yet he cared more than Thornton or Kay seemed to. She reached out and took his hand, squeezing it gently. "You...You didn't have to," she said as she tried to smile. "I'm...I'm fine." Samson frowned and shook his head. "I don't believe that." He turned his hand in hers and gave a squeeze of his own. "I don't." "Samson..." "You're their mate and they did something...something that upset you so much you ran. You wouldn't have run if you were fine." A low sound passed her lips and she felt more tears spill down her face. She looked away from him, unable to continue to look at the man who was obviously concerned about her wellbeing and wanted to help her. She wanted her mates to be the ones concerned and wanting to help. She wanted them to be the ones who had chased after her. She wanted...well, she supposed it didn't matter what she wanted. She'd wanted a happy mating with lots of love and acceptance. And look what she'd gotten. Maybe it was fate's way of further making her an oddity. It had already made her a weak and submissive she-wolf so why not give her the illusion of a happy mating only to snatch it away. Samson squeezed her hand again and made a low sound, a soft, gentle, comforting sound that immediately drew her gaze back to him. "You..." He paused clearly searching for the words. "You don't have to...talk...we could go for a run...hunt a rabbit or...or something." It was a natural pack response, to offer a run or hunt as a sign of comfort, and Kali started to say something, to politely say no maybe, but then stopped, a thought coming to her when she saw the soft, nearly unnoticeable look in Samson's eyes, it was a thought she hadn't considered until just that moment. Had anyone bothered to offer Samson that sort of comfort after the hunters had attacked? She had seen members of Thornton's pack leaning on each other, drawing comfort and strength from one another, but Samson had always seemed to be on the fringes. Pushed to the side to the point that he'd chosen to try and find comfort in the bottom of a bottle of alcohol instead of trying to reach out to someone because they just kept pushing him aside. Like he didn't matter. A soft sound, similar to the one he had made moments earlier, passed her lips and she gaze a nod."A run sounds...sounds great actually."

## Chapter Twelve

Kali ran with Samson for hours, chasing rabbits and playing tag with the Gamma who was as much an outsider in his own pack as she was in hers. When they parted ways, both to return to their respective packs, Kali had a momentary thought of *Why couldn't he have been my mate?* It was hardly a proud thought but it was honest, though she'd never give voice to it. Instead she'd said goodbye, promising to meet Samson again in a few days time, and headed home. The walk, since she hadn't had the foresight to bring her bicycle, was long and it gave her time to think. About her life. About her mates. About what she wanted. By the time she was walking up the front steps of her house she'd managed to work out a few things but not the really important ones. She supposed those would take some more thinking. She was as quiet as possible as she entered the house. It was late. No one would appreciate being woken up. She had just shrugged out of her jacket when the foyer light flipped on, startling her and making her whirl around with a faint growl, only to fall silent when she saw her father standing in the doorway leading to the kitchen. He did not look impressed."Where the hell have you been?" Nolan rumbled as he took a step towards her, his status of Beta nearly enough to make her bare her neck in submission but another instinct this one stronger than the first had her holding her ground. He was still her father but no longer was he her Beta. She was no longer part of the pack. "You're mother's been worried sick."She blinked in surprise.Before she could answer her mother's voice came from upstairs."Nolan? Nolan, is that Kali?" In the next heartbeat Renee was coming down the stairs, Kali looked at her mother, surprised by the whine that came from the woman, before Renee was off the stairs and pulling her into a hug. "Kali, oh thank God."Kali stood there, stunned, as her mother stepped back a bit, cupping her face between her hands. "Are you alright? What happened to your cheek?" Renee looked genuinely concerned and Kali felt her surprise at the situation melt away into confusion. What was going on? Why were her parents suddenly acting like she mattered? "Kali, honey, where have you been all day?""I...wha...I mean..." Kali couldn't seem to get a handle on her emotions. Everything just felt so wrong, like her world had tilted on its axis and wasn't about to right itself any time soon."Oh, is the freak finally home? Is everyone done panicking now?"Kali's gaze went to the top of the stairs where Chloe was leaning against the railing, sneering down at her. She bristled at the hated word from her sister but she didn't retaliate. Knew it wouldn't do any good since her parents would just chastise her for sinking to Chloe's level. Nolan growled in warning, which Chloe ignored as she made her way down the stairs, harsh gaze still fixed on Kali, but it was Renee who rounded on her eldest, fangs dropped and eyes glowing with her wolf. It was enough to make Chloe look reasonably scared and Kali watched her sister immediately tip her head, neck bared in deference to their mother's status as Beta."You will show some respect for your sister!" Renee's snarl was deep, more wolf than woman, and it added to Kali's confusion. She took a hurried step back, gaze darting back and forth from her mother to sister and then her father, who was merely watching things play out."Respect? For what?" Chloe scoffed and shook her head. "For a she-wolf who shows submission to any and everyone who yells at her? She's hardly worthy to be called my sister let alone a member of this family. She's weak! She's always been weak. If the pack were merciful they would have ended her a long time ago!"Kali felt a shiver of cold dread run up her spine. Centuries ago it had been common for a pack to exile or kill members who were deemed weak. It certainly gave her a new outlook on her sister if that was how Chloe thought she should have been dealt with. She took a small step back, survival instinct telling her to run, to get out of there before Chloe carried out that thinly veiled threat.Renee growled again and Nolan snarled Chloe's name but Chloe didn't seem to care."You both know she's weak," Chloe pressed on, looking from Renee to Nolan and then to Kali. "She doesn't deserve to be part of the pack. She'll get someone killed one day!"Kali stiffened as she looked at Chloe, really looked at her sister, seeing for the first time just how much Chloe really did despise her. The way her sister was looking at her reminded her far too much of the way her mates had looked at her. Like she was a problem. Like she was the one in the wrong. It caused a low growl to bubble up in her chest but she forced it back down.Chloe was wrong. Just like Thornton and Kay were wrong.She made a low sound. "I'm going to bed," she declared as she stepped towards the stairs, refusing to deal with any more of this tonight, she'd had her share of drama for the day.Chloe snarled. "Oh, no you're not, bitch," her sister spat, grabbing for her arm. "You're going to explain why Mum and Daddy had to wait up, worried about you, when your worthless ass was probably sulking somewhere in the woods because you've realized just how worthless you...ARGH!"Kali growled, her wolf pushing to the forefront her being, catching Chloe's wrist before her sister could touch her and used her grip to spin and throw her sister across the foyer. As Chloe hit the wall and slid to the floor Kali was barely aware of her father shouting her name, Renee telling her to calm down, that Chloe hadn't meant any harm. She growled again, deeper this time, glaring down at her sister like she'd seen Deucalion and Thornton do. It was an intimidation tactic. And either it or her sudden violent outburst, the first she'd ever shown, had Chloe sitting still as stone on the floor, staring up at her with wide eyes. "Listen to me, bitch," Kali spat as she continued to glare down at her sister. "I am tired. I am sick and tired of you running me into the dirt, of you constantly making me feel like shit just because I'm not like you and everybody else. Do you not think that I have feelings? Do you think that just because I'm different it doesn't hurt every time you or one of your asshole friends calls me a freak? You don't have to point it out, Chloe, I know I'm different. I've always known. And there is nothing to be done about that. But you know what? Someday, someday I might just find someone who doesn't care that I'm different. Someday I might find a place where I fit in. I might actually feel normal. But you? You will never stop being a heartless, selfish bitch!" Without another word or backwards glance Kali turned and raced up the stairs. She heard her mother call out to her but she didn't stop until she was in her room, the door slammed shut and locked behind her. She couldn't believe she'd just done that. For the first time in her life she had actually stood up to Chloe. A soft bubble of laughter escaped her as her collapsed onto the bed, sitting at the edge and staring at the far wall of the room without really seeing it. She'd finally stood up to her sister. And it had felt amazing. She knew there would be fallout from this. How could there not be? But for the first time since her mates had turned on her she felt like everything was going to be okay.

# Chapter Thirteen

Kali wasn't certain what had woken her. But one minute she was dead to the world and the next she was bolting upright in bed, looking around as though she expected something or someone to be there. She had a cold sense of dread rushing through her entire being and she clambered up from the bed. Something was wrong. Something was terribly wrong. Her neck ached and she reached up, fingers brushing over the mark there. "Kay," she whispered as she felt pain and fear filter through the bond she shared with her Beta mate, the bond she'd been blocking since fleeing Thornton's house a day ago. What she was feeling though was stronger than her ability to block the bond and it spurred her into action. Dressing quickly, a loose t-shirt and sweatpants, she stepped into her sneakers and glanced at her door. There was a chance her parents or sister was up and she couldn't take the chance of them seeing her and asking where she was going. Plus there was the chance that Chloe would want payback for what had happened between them the night before. Turning she rushed to the window, climbing out onto the roof she drew a deep breath and focused on her bond with Kay, trying to get a sense of where he was, of what was happening to him. She got the distinct impression of the forest, of rushing water and a massive tree. It was familiar and it took her a moment before she realized that what she saw and felt was familiar because she'd been there a dozen times. It just above the CherokeeFalls near a large oak tree. She'd been there just last night with Samson. Drawing a deep breath she used the garden lattice to climb down to the ground. From there she headed for the forest. She knew she could move faster in her wolf form but she wasn't certain what she was running to. Wasn't certain how useful her wolf would be. So she kept running, pushing herself, needing to get to Kay, to make certain he was alright. He might be angry with her, blaming her for something she didn't, wouldn't, do but he was still her mate. She had to be certain he was okay. Navigating the forest, taking paths she knew were quicker, she reached CherokeeFalls just as the sun was coming up. The water dulled her sense of smell but as she ran up the embankment leading to the top of the falls, to the tree she had seen, there was a scent too strong to be drowned out. Coopery and bitter. A warning bell went off in her head as she realized the scent of blood. Her fear intensified by she kept running. He mate was hurt, could possibly be dying, and the sooner she got to him the better. She knew she could be running straight into danger, could just as easily end up as hurt as Kay, but she couldn't just leave him to...to whatever was happening. As she reached the top of the falls she looked around, the tree was just to her right but where was Kay. A low sound drew her gaze to a patch of long grass and through the green and shadows she saw the grey and brown fur. "Kay," she murmured as she rushed forward, dropping to her knees next to the wolf, her mate, and felt tears brimming up in her eyes. Her mate's fur was matted with blood and there was a wound in his side. It was impossible for her to tell what had caused it or how serious it was but she knew he needed help and he needed it immediately. Their kind healed quickly but that wound was serious and he'd bleed out before he healed enough to get back to their pack on his own. "Hang on," she whispered, touching his head, his eyes opening and looking up at her. "Just hang on please. I'm going to get you home. I'm...I'm going to get you to Thornton." Kay whined, licking at her hand, and she felt the tears spill down her face as she carefully, slowly, lifted Kay into her arms. He was heavy but she managed to get to her feet, holding him close, he whined again and she felt anger battling with her fear but she pushed both down. Kay didn't need her fear or her anger. He needed her to be strong. For him she could be strong. She walked, slowly, not wanting to jar him, and with each step she could feel his blood soaking into her shirt, could feel it staining her arms and hands, sticky and warm and wet. It made her stomach roll and bile to rise into the back of her throat but she fought it down. Fought it down for Kay. Each step took her, took them, closer to Thornton. Closer to help.She was halfway to Lawton, halfway to Thornton and help, when the quiet of the forest was broken by a loud crackling bang, like a firework going off only louder and then pain, white hot fire licked at her left side, just below her ribs and it was enough that she stumbled forward, dropping to her knees, Kay yelping loudly as he fell from her arms to the ground. Gasping through the pain she looked down, watching as a stain bloomed on her shirt, spreading as the fabric soaked up the blood. Her blood.She blinked as fresh tears rolled down her face.She'd been shot.Looking around revealed no sign of the shooter. No sign of anyone.And while she was terrified she knew she had to get back up. Had to keep going.Kay made a low sound when she lifted him again, his eyes having dropped to her side, seeing the fresh stain, no doubt smelling her blood over his own. "It's okay," she gasped as she forced her body to move, to stand and walk, the pain licking up her side like fire. "We're going to be okay."It took longer, so much longer, for her to reach the backyard of Thornton's house and by then the pain and blood loss was starting to affect her. She made a low sound as she pushed herself into walking forward. Each step had fresh pain screaming through her and she stumbled as she neared the backdoor. She knew, with Kay in her arms, she wouldn't be able to open the door so she did the only thing she could think of. The only thing that made sense."Thornton!"She would have kicked at the door but the wound in her side made it difficult to stand, let alone shift her weight enough to do it, so she drew as deep a breath as she could manage and shouted her Alpha mate's name. She had just started to shout again when the door was suddenly, forcefully, yanked open and she was greeted by the sight of, not her mate, but a petite redheaded woman she recognized as Suzie, one of Thornton's Betas."What the...""Kay needs help," Kali said quickly, fighting through the pain to get the words out. "Please...help...""Jesus Christ on a pogo stick!" Suzie reached out, helping to support Kay's weight even as she stepped back, helping Kali carry him inside. "Table. Put him on the table."Kali nodded and together they managed to carefully, gently, lay Kay on the table before Suzie was shouting for Thornton, reaching for a dish towel to press against Kay's side, the wolf whining loudly, obviously in pain, and Kali's hands clenched before she was reaching out, lightly brushing back the fur on his face and neck. "It's okay," she whispered, leaning against the table as spots of grey began to dance through her vision. "It's...It's okay...""Kali?" Suzie's voice startled her and she looked at the other she-wolf. "Kali, honey, are you okay? Are you hurt?""I..." She looked down at Kay, his eyes had closed but he was still breathing, there was still a chance that he could be helped. "I'm fine...""You're pale." Suzie didn't sound convinced. "And shaking.""I just carried my mate...through the woods...all the way from CherokeeFalls..." Kali blinked, those spots in her vision slowly growing bigger. "I'm fine...just...just help Kay."At that moment Thornton, followed by three men she didn't recognize, all but stormed into the room. Thornton looked frantic and angry and concerned. "Oh god," he rushed to the table, hands covering Suzie's over the wound in Kay's side. He looked at one of his men and growled out "Go get the fucking doctor!" The man didn't hesitate and when Thornton looked at her, Kali wasn't sure what to do. "What happened?!" His snarl, the way he looked at her, it made her want to submit, to show her throat, but she held her ground, by sheer force of will she held her ground. "I don't know...I ...I just...I knew I had to find him." Thornton said nothing, his focus shifting completely to Kay, and while part of her was bothered that he hadn't asked if she was okay, she was just glad to have managed to get Kay here, to get him to help. She watched, in a bit of a daze, as Thornton and his men began tending to Kay. She felt Suzie touch her arm, heard the woman say something to step back, to give them room, and she seemed to act on autopilot as she stepped back. "Kali?" Suzie's voice suddenly sounded so far away, her vision tunnelling just as quickly, the grey spots growing until the world was dim and fading away. "Kali?" When the world tilted sharply she heard Suzie shout, felt the woman try to catch her, but it did little good as the floor suddenly rushed up to meet her. The last thing she heard before the darkness overtook her was someone shouting her name.

## Chapter Fourteen

"Kali? Kali, can you hear me?" The darkness she'd been cocooned in was slowly fading away. "Kali?" "Mr Crowe, just because she moved does not mean she is coming around. The painkillers will most likely keep her under for...Oh!" She blinked and squinted against the brightness, trying to lift her hand to block the light, she felt a tug in the back of her hand before someone was gently pushing her hand back down. "Easy, Kali." The voice, Samson's voice, caused her to blink again as she turned her head to look up at him. He looked beyond tired and worried and she wanted to reach up, to touch his cheek and ask him what was wrong but given that he was stopping her from moving it probably wasn't a good idea. "Sam...what..." "Miss Eldridge," the second voice, one she didn't recognize, caused her to look to her right, staring up at the face of a man with glasses and greying hair. "Miss Eldridge, I'm Doctor Kenneth Becket. Can you tell me how you're feeling?" She made a soft sound. "Groggy...my side...my side hurts..." Doctor Becket nodded. "The grogginess is from the painkillers and the fact that you lost consciousness due to blood lost," he said as he picked up what had to be her medical chart. "The pain, well, that is from the gunshot wound you sustained sometime before arriving at Alpha Garroway house." That suddenly had he thoughts turning from herself to the reason she was laying here. "Kay," she said as she looked from the doctor to Samson. "Where's..." "He's fine, Kali," Samson assured her as he reached up and brushed her hair back, reminding her that, once, he had been a father. "You got him help in time." Kali smiled, a little dopy, a by-product of the painkillers, and drew a deep breath, wincing as pain flared in her side when muscles pulled the wrong way. Samson's hand continued to comb through her hair. "It's alright," he said soothingly, giving her a small smile. "Once you can shift you'll be right as rain." Doctor Becket nodded his agreement. "You're exceedingly lucky, Miss Eldridge. Just a little bit more to the right and you..." "Is she awake?" The voice from the doorway caused Samson and Doctor Becket to both turn but Kali didn't need to try to sit up to know who it was. She knew Thornton's voice. Doctor Becket walked across the room and she heard him say something about her needing rest and that her mate should take care of her before Thornton let out a low rumbling sound. "I am her mate," the Alpha said lowly, and Kali's heart beat so hard against her ribs she was surprised that they didn't break. Hearing him say that, after what had happened between them, it hurt. Almost as badly as being shot had."Oh..." Doctor Becket suddenly sounded confused and embarrassed. "I thought...Mr Crowe he...he was here and..."Samson grunted. "I'm her friend, Doc." He slowly rose from where he'd been sitting on the edge of the bed, moving from her line of sight but she didn't have to see him to know he'd just put himself between the her and Thornton. It was the clearest sign a wolf could make, especially to his Alpha, to indicate which side he was taking."Oh..." The Doctor still sounded confused. "I just...I assumed...""I want to speak to my mate."Thornton's tone left no room for argument and Kali heard the Doctor leave but she could still scent Samson, could still see him, from the edge of her vision."Crowe. Out. Now."She heard Samson move, knew he was compelled by way Thornton had spoken, his tone completely Alpha but she also heard him pause, saying something softly, too softly for her to hear, but she heard Thornton's warning growl before footsteps and the door was slammed shut. She listened as footsteps approached the bed and Thornton came into view, he looked worn out and his shirt, a deep blue, was speckled with blood. Kay's blood, she realized as he looked down at her, his impossibly blue eyes flicking from her face to the IV in her arm back to her face. She stared right back at him."Kali..."He paused as though trying to find the words or trying to keep calm. She wasn't certain and she wasn't about to ask. Just looking at him, knowing what he thought of her, hurt."You saved Kay." His words washed over her and she frowned, the painkillers, still pumping through her IV, making it harder and harder to focus. "You...How did you know?" There was something in his tone, some question he wasn't asking, but she caught it. And she didn't like it. "You think...You think I hurt him?" When he said nothing she made a low sound. Hurt and anger and disbelief all rolled into one. "You think I...hurt Kay..." Tears prickled her eyes but she blinked them away. She'd shed enough tears for Thornton. "Kali..." "I...I got shot...trying to help my...our...mate." She felt her wolf shift beneath her skin, felt a growl bubbling up but she forced it down. "And you think...my God...you really hate me...don't you?" Thornton's expression changed but she still couldn't figure out what he was thinking or feeling. "Kali..." "Get out," she said as she closed her eyes, unable to look at him anymore. "Just...Just get...out..." She heard him move but didn't open her eyes. "Kali, we need..." His hand touched her arm and she snarled as her eyes flew open, jerking away from him which caused pain to flair but she ignored it, as much as she was able, instead focusing on him. "I said..." Her voice was more growl than actual words and she heard the door open, catching Samson's scent but remained focused on Thornton, who seemed surprised by her display of aggression. "Get. Out." "Kali..." "You heard her, Alpha," Samson snapped, suddenly appearing in Kali's line of sight. "Out." Thornton growled as he looked at Samson, clearly not impressed by his Beta's actions as Samson put himself between them once more. "This doesn't concern you, Crowe. This is..." "She's pack." Samson all but growled. "Her wellbeing is my concern. And right now I don't care if you're her mate or my Alpha. I care about her. And she told you to get out." Thornton snarled and started to step towards Samson only to stop when Doctor Becket snapped from the doorway. "Enough! I don't care what the hell is going out but Miss Eldridge needs peace and quiet! She needs rest! Now, if you can't manage that, I'm going to have to ask you to leave!" Kali thought, for a moment, that Thornton would argue, would use his status as an Alpha to refuse, but he gave one final, dark growl before turning and storming out of the room. Kali closed her eyes just as the tears finally slipped free, a low whine escaping her throat even as Samson was suddenly there, hand smoothing her hair back, whispering softly to her that everything was going to be alright. She wanted to believe him. She did. But she felt, not for the first time in the last few days, that her world was being tipped upside down and shaken like a snow globe.

# Chapter Fifteen

Kali sat, gingerly, on the couch in Samson's apartment and tugged at the strings of the borrowed jogging pants she was wearing. It had been a couple of hours since she'd been released from the clinic by Doctor Becket and only after she'd shifted, twice, just to convince the doctor that she was well enough to do so. Because her clothes had been covered in blood she'd had no other choice but to leave the clinic in her wolf form. Which hadn't been so bad, she supposed, at least she hadn't had to talk to Thornton, who stood in the hallway and watched as she'd left with Samson. Now here she was, sitting in Samson's apartment, wearing his clothes, though they didn't smell like him so there was a good chance that he had never worn them, and she had no idea what to do next. Part of her knew she should go home, she knew Kay was going to be alright and her parents had to have realized she wasn't there by now and were probably worried, but she just couldn't bring herself to do it. Her instincts kept telling her that she was where she was supposed to be. That she was with her pack. She knew part of that instinct was tied to the fact that she was mated to the pack's Alpha but it was also because she'd been accepted by the pack. It was as much hers as it was Thornton and Kay's. She had a duty here, one she didn't have in Henson, and, though she loved her family and friends, few as they were, there, she couldn't just give up her duty or pack. No matter what was happening between her and her mates. Drawing a slow breath she stood, hand pressed to the spot where she'd been shot because, despite healing when she'd shifted, it still hurt and pulled, and carefully made her way across the room, trying to figure out where the phone was so she could at least call her parents and let them know she was okay. Reaching a bookcase she paused, staring at a framed photograph, the only one she'd seen in the entire apartment. The photograph was old and faded but it had Kali's heart skipping a beat. It showed Samson hugging a girl who couldn't be anymore than eleven or twelve. His daughter, she thought as she looked at their smiling faces, at how happy Samson looked. The daughter who had been..."Her name was Annie." Kali startled and turned, finding Samson watching her from the doorway, his face unreadable but his eyes full of sadness. "Sam..." She watched as he crossed the room until he was standing next to her, reaching up to take the photograph down from the shelf, looking at with an expression full of hurt and regret. "She was eleven when this was taken," he said softly, his voice cracking ever so slightly as he ran his thumb over his daughter's face. "We'd just moved into the house. God she was so happy to finally have a yard. It was...It was two days before the hunters came..."Horror and sorrow swelled in her then as she realized that the last happy memory he had of his daughter was so clearly tainted by the pain of her loss. She reached out, wrapping her arms around his waist as she pressed her forehead to his shoulder, ignoring the way her side ached, needing to offer comfort to a man whose pain had clearly been overlooked by their pack. How had no one else seen this? How could they be so blind?She closed her eyes are tears prickled, knowing that this was why Samson drank so much, why he was always getting into fights. His grief was eating him alive. She didn't say anything, unable to find the words to properly tell him that he wasn't along, that she was there for him, but somehow he understood. In that silent way that only a pack member could."I wasn't home when they...when it happened..." He drew a stuttering breath and she knew he was fighting his own tears. "Was at work...but when word came...I've never run so hard before...but...I...I was too..."He let out a deep whining rumble, the sound bubbled up from his chest and Kali hugged him a little tighter."They had Shauna...my mate...in the yard. She was..." He made a pained sound as the memories seemed to overwhelm him for a moment and Kali wished she could take away all he'd suffered. Wished she could give him back his family. "She was trying to change...to shift...but...but they...there was so much blood and

Shauna she...I couldn't save her. I tore one of the hunters apart...the other...he ran...but I couldn't save my Shauna..." He turned his head, pressing his face into her hair, and she felt his tears dripping from his cheeks and she rumbled softly, trying to comfort him as best she could." The entire time I...I...could hear screaming and...I...didn't realize it was Annie until...until I could smell the smoke...feel the...the...heat of the flames..." Kali turned into his embrace fully, arms wrapping as tightly around him as she could, not wanting to hear anymore but knowing it was important that she listen. Samson had needed someone to listen for so long. She could be strong enough to do that. She could be a source of comfort and support when everyone else had just walked away." I tried...tried to get to the house but the fire...God...the fire was just...and then Kay was there...stopping me...he kept saying it was...it was too late...but I...I didn't believe him...even as I watched my house...burn...I didn't want to...think I'd failed my...my family..." "You didn't fail them." Kali spoke immediately, leaning up to nuzzle his neck in support and comfort, ignoring the sharp ache in her side. Her pain didn't matter right now. His did. He needed her right now." I did...I..." "Listen to me, Samson," she moved as she spoke, pulling back just enough to cup his face between her hands, forcing him to meet her gaze. When he tried to pull away she held tighter. "Listen!" He stilled immediately, whether because of her tone or her status as an Alpha Mate, but she didn't care. She just pressed on. "It was not your fault. It wasn't. You did everything you coul d.""It wasn't enough...""Sometimes it's not," she said softly, wiping his tears away with her thumbs. "Sometimes we do all that we can, push ourselves passed our breaking point, but it's not enough. But you can't keep living this way, Sam. Your family...Shauna and Annie wouldn't want you to do this to yourself."His expression was one of complete hopelessness and, for all the problems she and her mates were facing, she could imagine she'd cope much better than Samson had if something were to happen to Thornton or Kay. But she had to help him get off this self-destructive path before he did something terrible or before Thornton had enough and chased him from the pack."I don't know how...to...move on...""You take it one day at a time." She smiled, feeling her own tears prickle her eyes, but she blinked them away. He didn't need her tears right now. He needed her strength. Her reassurance and friendship. "You get up each day and say that it's going to be better. There's going to be bad days. But I'm here for you. I'm here to help you through the good and the bed."The soft, almost purr, that bubbled from his chest as he hugged her close said more than words ever would and as she hugged him she knew she'd made a difference. It might not be a huge or world altering difference but she'd done something to help a man, her friend, when he was in pain and no one else would listen or help. She'd done what she was supposed to. It was her role in the pack. To comfort and protect and help.Her heart leapt suddenly as something dawned on her.Everything she had just done, everything she wanted to do, to help and care for her pack, was all indicators of a wolf's rank. For her entire life she'd thought she would never have a rank, even her status as Alpha Mate wasn't the same, but her she was, realizing as she comforted and supported Samson, that she'd been so very wrong. She had a rank. She always had. She was an Omega.

## Chapter Sixteen

Kali sat in the cab of Samson's truck, staring up at the house she had grown up in, the only home she had ever really known. Her fingers gripped the steering wheel so tightly that her knuckles were turning white. Part of her wished that she'd accepted Samson's offer to come with her. But this was something she had to do alone. She was afraid, really afraid, of what would happen when she confronted her parents and she wished she had someone beside her for this. When she'd told Samson what she'd realized, that she was an Omega, he'd been surprised and confused, saying something about she should have known. That, unlike other wolves whose ranks typically manifested at birth, an Omega's rank was known the moment they were born. That her parents should have told her. She'd been both enraged and confused. Her parents had never told her anything about her rank and when she hadn't presented as a Beta like Chloe she'd always assumed it meant she was a Gamma. Most packs didn't have an Omega, only one in a thousand wolves was born Omega, so it never occurred to her that she was one. Even with all the traits that she had always thought made her a poor she-wolf she never guessed her true rank. She'd been so beaten down, by the pack and by her sister that she had just accepted that something was wrong with her. Drawing a deep breath she slowly climbed from the truck, pulling the borrowed jacket from Samson tighter around her. She had no idea what to expect when she went inside but she knew she had to face it head on. Because after today she would never be coming back. She was no longer part of the Henson Pack. She had finally accepted that. Walking up the driveway she took in the sight of the house, the yard, every inch of this place had a memory. Happy and sad. Good and bad. Entering the house she drew a deep breath, looking around, taking in the scents one last time before calling out. "Mom? Dad?" There was no reply and, after a heartbeat of listening, she realized that she was alone in the house. Sighing softly she walked up the stairs, remembering how as a child she'd run down them countless times, remembered how she'd sat at the top once and cried because Chloe was going to the prom and she wasn't. As she walked down the hallway she was surprised to see her bedroom door was open and, as she got closer, she realized it had been forced open because part of the doorframe was broken and another part was missing. Stepping into the doorway she was even more surprised to find her mother sitting on the bed amidst boxes. Renee was clearly crying and, in one hand, she held a framed photograph of the two of them. It had been taken during a family vacation to New York City. They had been in Central Park and her mother had swept her up into her arms next to the horse drawn carriage they'd ridden around in all afternoon, hugging and kissing her and calling her my special baby. It was one of the only times Kali remembered feeling normal. All because her mother hadn't treated her any different than Chloe. "I've always loved this picture," Renee said suddenly, running her hand over the glass before looking up at Kali, tears shimmering in her eyes but a small smile graced her face. "You were so happy that day. Laughing and smiling. It was wonderful." "You mean besides the fact that you lied to me for my entire life?" It was a crap thing to do, a Chloe thing to do, but she couldn't take the words back. "What? Kali, I don't..." "I'm an Omega." In any other situation the look on Renee's face would have made her laugh. But it just made her want to throw something, made her want to scream and rage, because it was clear that her knowledge of her rank was the last thing her mother had been expecting. "Kali..." "Would you ever have told me?" "Of course," Renee said as she stood, still clutching the photograph, tears spilling down her face. "Of course I would have. It was just...we decided you deserved to grow up as a normal wolf, without the...the pressure of being an Omega hanging over you." Kali's hands clenched at her sides and she resisted the urge to growl. "Normal? Normal?!" She knew she was all but screaming but she honestly couldn't bring herself to care. "You think the way I grew up was normal?! I thought I was a goddamn freak! I thought there was something wrong with me because I wasn't like you or Chloe or any other she-wolf! I grew up tormented because I was different! And you knew the whole time that I was suffering! And the kicker, mother, is that you could have stopped it by just telling me...by telling everyone...that I'm an Omega!" "Kali..." "And another thing," Kali couldn't help but growl as she gestured towards the boxes. "What the hell is all this?!" "Well," Renee said, reaching up to wipe tears away. "Your mate called and told us you'd been shot and that it made him realize that your place was with him and his pack and so you would staying with his pack and, I know this day was going to come but I..." "Wait, wait, wait!" Kali shook her head, certain she'd misheard her mother. "My what called?" Renee gave a watery smile as she set the photograph down, crossed the room and pulled the collar of the jacket aside, easily revealing one of Kali's mating bites. "Your mate, sweetheart."

## Chapter Seventeen

Kali returned to Lawton roughly an hour later, having spent the time packing and talking with her mother. And while she hadn't forgiven her mother for lying to her for her entire life, she had listened as Renee told her why they'd kept the truth of her rank from her. Her parents had seen, years before her birth, how an Omega had been treated, how, despite being such a crucial member of the pack, the poor man had suffered endlessly because his Alpha had treated him like a doormat because his natural instincts had been to protect and help the members of the pack, at any cost, even if it meant sacrificing his own life, which, in the end, was exactly what happened. Her parents had not wanted that to be her and, with help from their Alpha, they'd kept the truth from not only her but the entire pack. She sat outside Samson's apartment building, just sat in the truck, hands gripping the steering wheel so tightly that her knuckles were white and she felt tears prickle her eyes. She felt like her entire life had been nothing but a lie. She understood her parents and Alpha Deucalion wanting to protect her but they could have told her at least. Could have explained why it was so important that she keep the secret. She had the right to know her own rank. And that three people, three very important people in her life, had kept it from her both infuriated and saddened her. They hadn't trusted her and that, more than anything, hurt. Leaning forward she closed her eyes and rested her forward against the steering wheel, feeling the tears pooling in her eyes, a pained sound bubbled up from her chest and she tried to force all the hurt, the anger and disbelief, into a tiny corner of her mind. She knew she had to deal with it, work through it, but she just kept thinking of all the pain and anger and heartache she'd suffered. All the times she'd been bullied. All the times she'd been called freak or told there was something wrong with her. Her parents had tried to protect her, to keep her from sharing a similar fate to that of the Omega they had known, but in shielding her they had caused her the very suffering they had tried to spare her. She nearly jumped out of her skin when someone tapped at the window. Looking up she found Suzie standing beside the truck, looking concerned. Kali waited until the woman had stepped back before climbing from the truck. "Hey...Hey, Suzie," she said as she shut the door behind her, leaning back against the truck and hoping the female Beta wasn't here to pick a fight. Because in her current mood and state of mind she wasn't certain that she could be the passive she-wolf she had always been. "H eard through the grapevine you were moving in permanently," Suzie said, face completely unreadable and Kali fought down the urge to growl. She wasn't just some lowly pack member. She wasn't just some weak ass Omega. She was the Alpha Mate and if Suzie thought she was going to be walked all over than the Beta had another thought coming. "Didn't figure it would be to an apartment building halfway across town." Kali frowned. "What is that supposed to mean?" Suzie's expression finally opened up, becoming one of disbelief, and the other she-wolf's eyes widened. "You're the Alpha Mate, Kali," she said as though it should have all be completely obvious. "You...You're place is with Thornton. With Kay." Kali bristled. Apparently her Alpha mate hadn't told his pack what had happened between them. "My place," she snapped as her hands clenched at her sides, fighting down the urge to growl. "My place?! You may want to go ask Thornton about why I'm not living with him and Kay before you start talking about what my place is." Suzie frowned. "Kali...Kali whatever happened I'm sure Thornton is sorry and..." "I don't care how sorry he is!" Kali shook her head, feeling her wolf press upwards against her skin, claws prickling at her fingertips and fangs starting to slip down from her gums. "I could have died saving Kay and Thornton has the gall to think I had something to do with Kay being hurt in the first place! So he can go rot for all I care because I'm not living with him!" Suzie opened her mouth and closed it several times, looking much like a landed fish, but before she could say anything Samson was there, no doubt having seen them from the apartment and had come out to see what was going on. "Suzie," he said, voice deep and rumbling like thunder, causing the she-wolf to look at him sharply. "I think it's time you left." "This doesn't..." "If you say this doesn't concern me, Suzie, I'm going to put you into the dirt." Samson crossed his arms over his chest and stared her down. Gamma or not he wasn't backing down and, clearly, his actions surprised Suzie because she took a small step back, staring at him with wide eyed curiosity. "Now get going. Kali needs to get settled in." Suzie nodded though she looked at Kali, waiting for her fellow she-wolf to nod, before she finally turned and headed off down the street. Samson waited until she was far enough away before turning his attention to Kali, reaching out to lightly touch her arm. "Are you okay," he asked as she looked up at him. "You're pale. Really pale." "I'm...I'm fine," Kali said, though she wasn't certain if she was trying to convince him or herself. "Just...Just a little shaken up." "After everything you've been through in the last twenty-four hours I think you're allowed to be a little shaken up." She chuckled and leaned into his touch, thankful that she had someone who was on her side. Because she had a feeling that she was going to need someone in her corner in the coming days.

## Chapter Eighteen

Weeks passed and Kali quickly found herself settling in rather nicely in Lawton. She got a job at a local bar and while waiting tables was drastically different than working at a bookshop had been she found she enjoyed it much more. It gave her a chance to truly interact with people. People who didn't treat her like there was something wrong with her. It was a wonderful and very welcomed changed.

Working at the bar also gave her the ability to watch over Samson, to ensure he didn't overstep his limits, but it seemed that having someone living with him, having someone to look out for, had helped curb the majority of his drinking issues.

She was working one afternoon when the bar was fairly quiet, only a handful of folk in for lunch, and had just finished wiping down a table when the door opened, a gust of wind rushing in, causing people to grumble against the unexpected chill. But with the wind came a scent, a very familiar scent, and Kali closed her eyes for a moment. A single name whispering through her mind.

Kay.

It was the first time since he'd been shot that she'd scented him.

Slowly turning she watched as his gaze swept the room before finding her.

Despite the warmth in his eyes she wasn't certain that she could handle speaking to him. She could still remember him just standing there as Thornton had accused her of cheating, of betraying their bond, and, even though he hadn't come right out and accused her to, even though she had risked her life to save his, he had still hurt her. And, even if it was petty of her, she wasn't ready to deal with that yet. Not when she'd finally started to get control of her life.

So she turned and headed back towards the bar.

She had just stepped around behind it, had just laid her cleaning cloth on the little shelf beneath the bar, when Kay was suddenly there. This close, only the width of the bar separating them, his scent washed over her like a wave and she shivered despite herself. Her every instinct screaming that her mate needed her. That he'd come here for her. She violently pushed those instincts away.

"Hey," he said as he smiled at her, a sweet, charming, upturn of his lips that had her heart skipping several beats.

"Can I help you," she asked politely, thinking it might be easier to treat Kay as just another customer instead of as her mate.

Kay didn't seem surprised by her reaction to him.

The look in his eyes told her that he'd been expecting something much worse.

"How are you?"

She blinked.

"I'm fine."

She really didn't know what else to say.

Kay gave a slight nod. "Thornton told me you were shot when you saved me."

She drew a slow, deep breath, remembering the fiery pain of the bullet ripping through her. How weak she'd grown, the more blood she'd lost, but she also remembered how strong she'd been, how determined she'd been to save him. She gave a slow nod.

"I suppose I did." She gave him a searching look. "Did he also tell you he accused me of having something to do with you being hurt?"

He couldn't mask his surprise in time and she huffed before shaking her head.

"I didn't think so."

She started to turn, thinking to find something in the backroom to do until Kay left, but her mate reached across the bar, catching her arm and pulling her to a stop. She gave his hand a withering look and, before she could say anything, caught movement from the corner of her eye, having to wave Carter, the bouncer, back to his stool. The big Beta fixed Kay with a cold glare before settling back down.

"Kay, let go of me, now," she put just a hint of growl behind her words and was somewhat amazed when her mate listened to her. "Look, just in case you missed the subtle hint, let me lay it out for you. Leave. Me. Alone."

"Kali..."

She started to walk away again and wasn't really surprised when Kay caught her arm again.

"Kali, please, please I just...I want to talk...please, I'm sorry for being a dick. I..."

Before Kay could say anything else Carter was there, one hand clamping down hard on the Lead Beta's shoulder, a deep growl rumbling from his chest.

"Out."

It was all Carter said but it was enough to make Kay growl in response.

"This doesn't concern..."

"I don't care that you're Lead Beta or an Alpha Mate. You're harassing one of my mate's employees," Carter got right in Kay's face as he spoke, eyes shifting to wolf ever so slightly. "Not to mention my friend. So, if you want to keep the hand, Yorke, I suggest you let go now."

"You..."

Carter growled, his free hand shooting out to ensnare Kay's wrist, grip brutally tight. It was enough that, even as her mate gasped in pain, Kay reflexively released Kali's arm.

"Now," Carter rumbled. "You're going to leave, quietly, or I'm going to drag you outback and teach you how to properly treat a lady. You hear me, Yorke?"

Kay looked at Kali, gaze almost pleading, but she was still too angry with him, too upset by the entire situation, and she merely turned and walked away, into the backroom, hearing Carter tell Kay to way as the door swung closed behind her.

Once out of sight of the patrons of the bar she let out a shaky breath and leaned back against the wall, rubbing a hand over her face. A hand that trembled and it took her a minute to realize she was shaking. She forced herself to draw a deep breath, closing her eyes and concentrating on calming the rapid beat of her heart. She nearly jumped out of her skin when someone touched her shoulder, her eyes flying open even as her wolf tried to surge through to the forefront.

She blinked when she realized it was just Carter.

"God, Carter," she chuckled softly, shaking her head. "You scared the daylights out of me."

"Sorry, pup," he said, voice deep and rumbling but in a warmer way than when he'd spoken to Kay. "Just wanted to make sure you're okay."

Kali forced a smile even as she gave a nod. "I'm fine, really."

Carter frowned, reaching up to tuck her hair behind her ear. "You need to learn to lie better, pup."

Kali couldn't help but chuckle.

He was probably right.

"I'll be okay, Carter," she answered honestly. "Just...Just going to take some time, I guess."

Carter gave her a soft look. Which seemed so at odds with the rough Beta she'd gotten to know since starting at the bar.

"You take your break early," he said as he stepped towards the door. "I'll keep an eye on things."

"Carter..."

"Ain't a suggestion, pup," the Beta said with a look that said he wouldn't take no for an answer. "You take that break. I'll see you in fifteen."

Without another word he stepped back out into the bar and Kali sighed softly, sliding down the wall until she was sitting on the floor. She hung her head, burying her fingers in her hair and wishing she didn't feel all tied up in knots just because she'd seen Kay.

## Chapter Nineteen

Kali didn't see or hear from either of her mates for a week and, before she knew it, it was time for the full moon gathering. She was nervous and jittery and though Samson and Carter, and Carter's mate, Lydia, tried to give her as much comfort as they could it didn't really help. But she sucked it up, reminding herself of everything she'd already survived, and went with Samson to the spot in the forest where the pack was gathering.

It wasn't much different than the spot where the Henson Pack met.

It was a meeting circle, much like the one she'd grown up going to, just situated nearer the falls and slightly smaller.

Samson walked along beside her, ever the loyal friend and protective Gamma. People glanced at her as she passed, which was no different than her birth pack had been, but now they didn't look at her with scorn or disgust. Now she only saw respect. Because these wolves knew who she was. She was an Omega and an Alpha Mate. And even if she hadn't been an Alpha Mate her status as an Omega, with the Lawton Pack at least, afforded her the respect of her pack.

Normally, as an Alpha Mate, she would have gone to stand next to Thornton and Kay, who were already at the head of the group, but given everything that had happened between them, all her hurt and anger, she stayed with Samson and wasn't surprised when Carter and Lydia joined them. She saw Kay look at her, saw the longing in his gaze, but when Thornton looked at her she wouldn't meet his gaze, would barely look at him. When her Alpha mate realized she wasn't going to be joining him and Kay he slowly made his way to the center of circle.

And, despite everything, Kali politely bowed her head in respect of Thornton's position just as the rest of the pack did.

"Welcome, my friends," Thornton's voice boomed through the air and Kali pretended she didn't shiver in response to it. "Another full moon, another night to run as a pack, we are truly blessed." People nodded and murmured their agreements even as Thornton smiled. "Tonight I wish you safety, I wish you peace and I wish you fun." There was laughter and Thornton's smile widened. "Now, let's run."

People howled and cheered and Kali almost laughed at the big, dopey grin on Carter's face. Lydia rolled her eyes at her mate's expression before giving Kali a look that clearly said what can you do before they all walked off into the trees. Kali was aware, keenly aware, of Kay and Thornton watching her but she ignored them.

Once a short distance away from the circle Kali stepped behind a large tree and stripped. She still wasn't comfortable with changing forms in front of others and, thankfully, her friends understood and accepted that. She left her clothes tucked beneath some undergrowth before stepping back. Gooseflesh broke out over her skin but she ignored that as she focused on the change. On her wolf. She felt the change overtake her, felt her human form slip away and soon she stood as a wolf.

She shook herself, getting rid of the lingering tingles of the change, before stepping back around the tree to rejoin her friends who were also in their wolf forms.

Carter's wolf was massive, not nearly as big as Thornton but pretty close, and his fur was a dark rusty color. Next to him Lydia looked even tinier. Her silvery grey fur stood out vividly against Carter's darkness. But what truly surprised her was Samson.

Where once his wolf had been lean and lanky, looking malnourished and his fur matted and dirty now he looked healthier, though perhaps not as bulky as he should be, and his fur was well groomed and a beautiful glossy grey-black. It was how the Gamma had looked before the loss of his mate and child. And Kali didn't need to even think about why Samson looked so much better.

Samson had needed a purpose in his life, had needed something to drive him back into the land of the living, and he had found it in her. And maybe, now that the pack was starting to see him, truly see him, maybe he would find it in the people he had known and cared about for years.

With a soft yip Kali took off like a shot into the forest, hearing Samson howl and Carter and Lydia bark as they gave chase.

Kali had never experienced anything like running with other wolves.

Her entire life she'd had to run alone, out of fear, but now she was free to run with her friends, her pack. She leapt over a fallen log and had just rounded a tree when a howl caught her attention and she skidded to a stop, nearly being run over by Carter in process. The big Beta immediately licked at her ears in apology and she bumped his shoulder before she looked around them, listening intently until, distantly, she heard that howl again.

Thornton.

Her mate was calling to her.

She shifted about for a moment, torn about what to do, but then she shook her head and turned in the opposite direction. Her friends followed her loyally. They reached the rocky terrain that led up to the top of Cherokee Falls. They took time to drink, to rest, though Carter kept jumping at Samson, trying to coax the smaller male into playing.

Kali huffed as she laid in the long grass, Lydia next to her, both she-wolves watching as Carter finally seemed to convince Samson to tussle with him.

Lydia let out a soft chuffing sound, laughing at her mate and friend, while Kali alternated between watching the two play and keeping an ear and nose out for trouble. While they were still on Lawton Pack land they were still close to the boundary line and, though nothing had happened between the two packs yet, she would never put it passed the younger wolves, her sister included, to try something just to show off or prove they weren't cowards.

Wolves, no matter their rank, could be stupid creatures like that sometimes.

Minutes ticked away and Kali had just started to relax, had started to think that perhaps nothing was going to happen, that she'd been worried for nothing, when a twig snapped and her head turned immediately. Her fur bristled and low warning growl bubbled up from her chest as she caught sight of the slender grey she-wolf approaching with a small group fanned out around her.

Even without scenting the air Kali knew that wolf.

She'd been tormented by it her entire life.

Chloe.

And nothing in her sister's posture suggested she was there to be friendly.

## Chapter Twenty

Kali was on her feet even as her sister growled.

She wasn't surprised when Carter and Samson flanked her, the two males showing their teeth and Carter drawing himself up to full height, using his status as a Beta to try and force Chloe and the others to back down. Kali knew it wouldn't work. Her sister wouldn't realize the danger she was in. The danger she was leading her friends into. There were seven, no, eight, opposing wolves and Kali knew that in a fight, no matter how big Carter was or how fiercely Samson fought, they'd be outmatched.

There was only one choice.

She threw her head back and howled even as she finally opened up the bonds she shared with her mates.

She felt the immediate flood of shock, relief and joy, none of it her own, but pushed it down as she focused on her still advancing sister. She just needed her mates to use the bond to find them, to bring more of the pack, but she was starting to think there wasn't time for that.

Chloe growled deeply and bared her fangs, tail lifting, her stance firm and it made Kali growl in response.

Her sister was not above her.

Not here. Not on Lawton land.

Here she was not the submissive little she-wolf she'd grown up as.

Here she was not Chloe's victim.

Here she was an Alpha Mate.

Here she was a true she-wolf.

And she was not backing down from her sister.

Not now. Not ever again.

Instead she took Chloe by surprise and met her bitch of a sister head on.

They came together in a clash of fangs and claws, snarls and growls and savage rumbles filling the air even as, around them, their allies watched, stunned, at least until one of Chloe's group decided to try and join the fight and Samson leapt in to stop him. After that things went to hell in a hand basket. But as concerned for her friends as Kali was she never took her attention from Chloe. She knew if she did then she'd be dead. Chloe wasn't playing this time. This time her sister meant to kill.

Again and again the two she-wolves came together.

Biting, clawing and snarling.

Chloe kept trying to go low, to sink her teeth into Kali's belly, but weeks of roughhousing with Samson had taught Kali new tricks and she used them. Feinting left and then striking from the right. Chloe countered rather well and Kali knew she had to find some way of turning the fight in her favour before anything happened to her friends.

And then the idea came to her.

She could hear the rush of the water, feel the rocks beneath her paws and knew what to do.

Snarling she leapt to the right, goading Chloe into following her and, as her sister lunged, jaws open, intent clear, Kali dropped to the ground and rolled away. Chloe yelped as she slammed into the rocks, slipping and sliding along the wet stones and ending up half in the creek. She yelped again and scrambled, trying to get her footing under her but Kali was there, jaws closing around the back of her sister's neck, holding tightly, fangs piercing the skin, drawing blood, the taste thick and coppery in her mouth and, when Chloe started to move, to try and break free, Kali growled and shook her head slightly in warning.

Chloe growled and started to move again only to yelp in surprise and pain when Kali unexpectedly drug her away from the bank, using the momentum to throw Chloe across the ground, watching her roll, and pouncing the moment Chloe landed on her back, jaws once more closing around her sister's flesh.

This time around the bitch's throat.

Everything around them fell still and silent.

From the corner of her eye she saw Lydia scramble away from one of Chloe's friends even as Carter grabbed the smaller male by the scruff and tossed him several feet away from his mate. Samson had a sandy brown she-wolf pinned and, judging from the amount of blood spilling onto the ground around her head said she-wolf was either dead or dying. The rest, though still outnumbering Kali and the others, were backing down. They had followed Chloe and now Chloe was pinned, in a submissive position, beneath the she-wolf everyone in the Henson Pack had thought too weak to ever be a real threat.

Kali growled again even as her sister whimpered and she looked at the wolves who were still stepping back, though one, a lanky tawny male was crouched low, tail tucked beneath his belly and, when Samson looked at him, whined loudly and quivered. She didn't understand that but thought, perhaps, that it was just fear. Returning her attention to her sister she gave Chloe a slight shake, the meaning clear, before slowly releasing her, stepping back and waiting for Chloe to shift back to her human form before she herself shifted.

"Did you seriously think you'd accomplish whatever you came to do," Kali snarled, eyes blazing, her wolf still very much at the forefront. "Did you seriously think you wouldn't be caught?!"

Chloe growled faintly and, in response, Kali felt her claws pop out and her fangs drop.

"I didn't think you'd be running with back up," Chloe spat, her gaze still murderous despite the fact that she'd just submitted, in front of witnesses, to her younger sister. "Thought you'd be alone. Thought I could..."

"Kill an Alpha's mate."

Kali's head turned at the sound of Thornton's voice and she watched him, Kay and a dozen or more others approach, fanning out around them. The way Chloe looked at Thornton had Kali snarling and stepping towards her sister. She didn't care if she and her mates were having problems. No one, not even her sister, got to look at Thornton, or Kay, the way Chloe was.

She would have likely clawed Chloe's eyes out but Kay was, surprisingly and suddenly at her side, his palm sweeping lightly over the small of her back and, though she knew they still had things to work out, she took a bit of comfort from his presence. She let it be a balm against the fury her sister had riled within her.

"I have every right to kill you, all of you," Thornton rumbled as his Betas and Gammas surrounded Chloe's friends. All but the tawny male who was still curled up on the ground, watching Samson and only Samson. "For trespassing and for threatening my mate and pack. But I might be willing to show you mercy if you tell me why you attacked my mate."

Chloe let out a low sound, something between a chuff and a whine, and Kali started to take another step forward but still when Lydia suddenly appeared at her side, her friend taking hold of her hand, lacing their fingers together, the smaller she-wolf glaring at Chloe darkly.

"She took what should have been mine!"

Chloe's words were cold yet whiny and Kali blinked, some of her wolf receding as confusion began to fill her. What on earth was Chloe talking about? Thornton, it seemed, shared her thoughts because her Alpha mate gave Chloe an unreadable look before huffing lightly.

"And what," he growled. "Is it she's meant to have taken?"

"You!" Chloe's voice had risen to a shout and Kali's confusion quickly turned to shock. "You should have been my mate! Not that useless freak's! Mine!"

## Chapter Twenty-One

Kali blinked.

And then Chloe's words fully sank in and she snarled.

"What?!" She started to step forward but again Kay pulled her to a stop. "You think...You...Are you insane?!"

Chloe glared at her and Kali growled.

"I've been the perfect she-wolf," Chloe growled, eyes blazing, shining with a hint of her wolf. "Strong. Beautiful. Powerful." Her gaze narrowed. "If anyone deserved an Alpha mate it was me! Not you! I knew if I could just get rid of the two of you then I could woo Alpha Garroway and he'd see that I am the perfect mate. That I'm worthy of leading a pack at his side."

Thornton growled suddenly, drawing Chloe's gaze even as other members of the Lawton pack glared at her, their postures tense, some were flexing their claws. All ready to rip her apart for her threat to the Alpha Mates of their pack.

"The two of them," Thornton question, voice pitched low, dark and the rumble in his voice was full of his power as Alpha. "Were you planning on targeting Kay tonight as well?"

Chloe let out a low sound and shot Kay a disgusted look.

"If Ryan had done the job right he'd already be dead. Same as that little bitch. Stupid shit never did know how to handle his daddy's rifle right."

A collective growl went through the pack and Kali felt her heart try and crawl into her throat. Her sister had just admitted to having had one of her friends shoot Kay and then her. All because in her crazy mind she believed that Kali had stolen something from her. Something that had never truly been hers. Fate had given Kali to Thornton and Kay, just as it had given them to her. Something must have come loose in Chloe's brain. Something important.

Kali snarled, deep and dark, her wolf pressing up from deep within her and, wrenching free of Kay's hold, she launched herself at her sister, shifting in midair.

Chloe shrieked as Kali slammed into her, trying to shift, fighting to get away, but Kali was full of rage. Rage that her own sister had tried to kill her, had nearly killed her mate, all because of a delusion that Kali's Alpha was supposed to be hers.

Her claws and fangs sank into vulnerable human flesh and Chloe screamed as Kali tasted blood, her wolf driving her, pushing her to eliminate the threat to her mates, to her pack.

Before she could go for the suffocating bite, the killing bite, to Chloe's throat, a hand grasped tightly into the scruff of her neck, jerking her back. She twisted and snapped at the hand reflexively. Feeling an echo of pain in her front left paw before she realized that Thornton was the one who had grabbed her. Thornton had stopped her from killing her sister. Something that, while she wanted in her rage induced state, she knew she would feel guilty about for the rest of her life if she had actually gone through with it.

Whining faintly she licked at Thornton's hand in apology and was surprised when his expression softened, grip loosening on her fur, fingers gently combing through the soft white tuffs before he stepped away, moving towards Chloe. His body language said what he himself did not.

He was Alpha.

It was his duty, his right, to kill the threat to his mates and pack.

Kali stepped back, remaining in her wolf form, watching Chloe closely as her sister, now badly wounded, tried to push herself backwards across the ground. Trying to get away from the Alpha she had clearly pissed off.

A low growl bubbled up from Kali's chest and it tapered off only when Kay crouched next to her, running his hand over her side, smoothing down the fur that was still standing on end.

Despite the sick twist in her stomach she forced herself to watch as Thornton, claws extending from his fingertips, slashed open Chloe's throat.

It was the only way.

So she would know, so her wolf would know, the threat was truly gone.

Thornton stood over Chloe until she was dead and then he turned to the members of his pack who were now holding Chloe's friends and accomplices.

"Take them, and the bodies, into town," he rumbled, eyes blazing with his status of Alpha. "I'll contact their Alpha and he can deal with them."

As Chloe's friends were hauled away Kali noticed that Samson was still standing over the tawny wolf, neither moved, not even when Thornton let out a low growl, attempting to get Samson's attention.

The Gamma briefly glanced at his Alpha but pressed closer to the tawny wolf, who curled tighter into a ball, his body language and scent reeking of submission.

Kali scented the air even as Thornton rumbled in warning to Samson's clear defiance. It took her a moment but she managed to sort the tawny wolf's scent from the others and she shifted quickly, eyes wide as the small male looked at her with wide, frightened eyes. She let out a soft, disbelieving sound even as she spoke the wolf's name.

"Ephraim?"

## Chapter Twenty-Two

Kali sat in the living room of Thornton's house, curled up on the couch next to a boy she had known nearly all her life.

Ephraim Mallard was the youngest brother of Chloe's friend Ryan, the one who had shot Kay, and he had always been such a sweet boy. A few years younger than herself he was kind and generous and because of that Ryan, and everyone the Beta had associated with, Chloe included, had bullied Ephraim. Kali honestly couldn't remember Ephraim ever fighting back. He just took each beating or insult and carried on.

It made her sick to know that Ryan had forced Ephraim into helping him and Chloe.

And she knew he had because she'd cornered him once the pack had locked him in the cells beneath town hall, threatening to castrate him, with her fangs, if he didn't tell her the truth.

It was the reason Ephraim was with her and not locked up with the others.

Well, that and the fact that Samson had, quite literally, pulled Thornton aside when the Alpha had tried to order the boy be placed with the others. She hadn't been able to hear what Samson had said, saw old the wild gestures in Ephraim's direction, but she'd seen the shock on Thornton's face and had a pretty good idea what was going on. But instead of dwelling on that she remained focused on Ephraim.

He was quiet and shaking and looked absolutely terrified. Especially since Samson was standing on the other side of the room, watching him intently, eyes blazing with his wolf.

Shaking her head but unable to bring herself to tell Samson to back off or go in another room she reached up and pulled the quilt off the back of the couch, gently wrapping it around Ephraim, who jerked slightly and stared at her with wide, frightened eyes.

"It's okay, Ephraim," she said softly. "Nothing is going to happen to you. I promise."

Ephraim let out a soft whine and shook his head even as he pulled the quilt tighter around his shaking shoulders. "But I...I...I attacked you...I..."

"Ephraim," Kali reached up, gently cupping his cheek, not surprised that he flinched, wishing she could take away his fear, wishing she could wipe away every bruise and hurt. He was a good person. He didn't deserve everything that had happened to him. "Sweetie, Ryan told me everything. What he threatened if...if you didn't go along with Chloe's plan."

Ephraim whined again, the sound full of fear, and Kali saw Samson twitch in response but she quickly wrapped her arms around the boy, hugging him tightly, trying to convey nothing but kindness and comfort.

"It's going to be okay, Ephraim," she whispered in his ear as she gently brushed his hair back, seeing Kay step into the room out of the corner of her eye. "I promise."

He whined, loudly, and leaned into her, face pressed against her shoulder and she gently rocked him when he started to cry. She kept whispering that it was going to be okay, that she was sorry she hadn't been able to protect him before but she would protect him from now on and, after a while, his breathing evened out as he slipped into a fitful sleep.

Moving slowly she gently lowered him to the couch, tugging the quilt around him so it covered him better and tucked a pillow beneath his head. The moment she stepped back Samson was there, kneeling next to the couch, hand gently running over Ephraim's hair, murmuring softly. Kali smiled and slowly turned away, crossing to where Kay was still lingering in the door way.

As she reached her Beta mate she saw his curious expression. "Are they..." he started, nodding towards Samson and Ephraim and she gave a slight shrug, wrapping her arms around herself.

"Probably." She bumped her shoulder gently against his shoulder as she passed him on her way into the kitchen, knowing he'd take the hint and follow her.

Once in the kitchen she wasn't surprised when Kay suddenly wrapped his arms around her, pulling her back against him.

"Kay..."

"Was so fucking scared out there," he whispered against her hair. "Thought...Kept thinking something was going to happen to you. That I...That I was going to lose you before I could tell you how sorry I was for being such a prick to you about...about what Shawna told us."

Kali rumbled faintly and started to pull away, wounds opening again at the reminder of her mates' doubt in her, but Kay wasn't about to let her go. Not yet.

"Shawna told us everything after she saw what Thornton did to your sister," he said, nuzzling at her hair. "She told us Chloe paid her, gave her the photos. Guess she was afraid of meeting the same fate if we learned the truth on our own."

Kali let out a low whimper.

"Did...Did she say why did agreed to do it?"

"The money. She had debts, debts no one knew about, and she figured it would be a way to wipe her slate clean." Kay hugged her a little tighter. "Thornton banished her from the pack. I thought...he looked like he wanted to rip her head off. And I...I'm so sorry, Kali. I'm sorry I didn't trust in you. I'm sorry I didn't at least ask...press...about the issue."

Kali let out a soft sound as she reached up and covered Kay's hands with her own.

"The man...in the photos...he's my friend Amy's mate," she said softly, not hearing when Thorton walked into the kitchen. "He...He'd just told me they were going to have their first baby." She felt tears prickle her eyes. "Amy and Roy were the only people who never treated me different. They...They were my only friends. I'm sorry you thought..."

"No."

Thornton's voice startled her and she nearly jerked out of Kay's arms.

She watched, warily, as her Alpha mate approached her, his gaze soft and, when he reached up to cup her face between his hands, she barely kept from flinching, remembering how angry he'd been, how he'd all but accused her of hurting Kay.

"You have nothing to be sorry for," the Alpha said gently. "We're...I am sorry. For not listening. For not trusting. I let my anger and jealousy and fear cloud my judgement. And I'm sorry for everything, Kali. I...I will spend the rest of my life trying to earn your forgiveness. Making things up to you."

Kali felt the tears spill down her face. "Thornton..."

He pressed a kiss to her forehead.

"There are not words enough for how sorry I...we...are, Kali," Thornton said, giving her a soft look, wiping her tears away as Kay nuzzled at her hair, then her neck, trying to calm and comfort her. "But I promise we will do whatever it takes to make this right."

Kali let out a soft huff of breath, nearly laughing, and shook her head, mindful not to hit Kay whose head was resting in the slope of her neck.

"Just...Just hearing you say you're sorry is...is more than enough," she said, fresh tears spilling down her face. "You...You are...This is the first time someone's ever apologized to me and really meant it."

She saw Thornton's eye widened and suddenly she was being embraced, tightly, by both her mates. Both kept talking, trying to be heard over the other, apologizing and promising to do better, to be better, to never hurt her again. And all the while she stood there and cried, clinging to Thornton with one hand and Kay with the other.

She didn't know what the future held but, for the first time in a long time, she felt like things were going to be alright.

# EPILOGUE

..One Month Later...

Kali stood in the gathering circle, the full moon shining through the leaves of the trees above, and she smiled as she glanced at her Alpha, one of her mates, as he stepped up to address the pack.

As he welcomed them, thanking them for their continued support of him as leader, wishing them safety and happiness on the night of the moon, she smiled.

Thornton was a leader not only because he was Alpha but because he had the love and respect of his people.

To her left Kay rumbled happily and she glanced at her Beta mate, still smiling, squeezing his hand as their pack cheered and howled, some stripping and shifting right there, others moving off into the trees. She spotted Samson in the crowd and saw he was alone. Meaning

Ephraim was still not comfortable in being around the pack. She knew it would take time for the young man, little more than a boy really, to fully accept his place and status among his new pack but she knew Samson was patient enough for the both of them. Eventually Ephraim would realize how accepted and cared for he would be among the Lawton wolves.

Giving Samson a nod when he smiled and waved at her she turned with Kay and walked off into the trees, Thornton right behind them.

She had overcome some of her shyness when it came to changing forms but she still wasn't comfortable enough to do it in front of anyone but her mates and, as she stripped out of her clothing, she heard both rumble appreciatively. She giggled faintly as she let the change overcome her. Her wolf's joy was as much her own as human skin melted away to fur and claws and fangs.

Shaking after the lingering effects of the change she had just started to turn, to face her mates, when Thornton, already in his wolf form tackled her. They rolled across the ground and she yipped playfully while he nipped gently at her ears.

When they stopped rolling she bucked, scrambling to get her feet under her and, once she managed to wiggle her way out from beneath Thornton's bulk she bolted off through the underbrush. She heard Thornton, and Kay, giving chase and chuffed as she leapt over a fallen tree, turning on a dime the moment her paws hit the ground and, darting towards a large maple tree, she changed from wolf to woman, ducking around the tree, pressing her back against it just as her mates came crashing through the brush.

She smiled as she listened to them slow, listened to the scent the ground and air, but then everything went quiet. Too quiet.

Smile dipping slightly she leaned around the tree, searching for her mates, but saw nothing.

Where had they gone? And why hadn't she heard them?

Turning, she started to move, thinking to draw them out, only to let out a startled shout as she came face to face with Thornton, who had, at some point, shifted forms and, before she could dart backwards he grabbed hold of her, lifting her before rolling her to the ground, pinning her beneath him. She laughed as he nuzzled at her neck, mouthing at the mating mark he had graced her with when they had first mated and suddenly he growled and jerked.

She blinked and quickly realized Kay, also back in his human form, was crouching behind Thornton, nipping, albeit gently, at the back of the Alpha's shoulder.

"Brat," Thornton rumbled but smiled lovingly as Kay leaned up to nuzzle at his cheek.

"You love it," Kay replied cheekily, winking down at Kali, making her giggle, which brought Thornton's attention back to her and she all but purred when he moved against her.

"Thornton...Kay..."

"Hush, darling," Kay grinned as he reached around Thornton, running his hand teasingly over Kali's hip. "We've got the whole night ahead of us."

Thornton chuckled, kissing his way up Kali's neck. "And we're just getting started."

Kali rumbled and knew they'd make good on that promise.

Her heart soared and she thanked fate for giving her this life. For giving her these two wonderful men as her mates.

It was more than she could ever have asked for.

www.ingramcontent.com/pod-product-compliance
Lightning Source LLC
Chambersburg PA
CBHW070952080526
44587CB00015B/2275